"*Glow Up* could not come at a better time when today's girls are searching for truth and validation. Brittany addresses the lies our girls believe and equips them with God's truths. Brittany is your ultimate hype girl, championing the next generation to question the negative committee camping out between their ears. Her stories are relatable, raw, and authentic. Brittany's book is hilariously funny, drawing you in from page one and making you feel like you are in the presence of your very best friend."

—**Trudy Lonesky,** best-selling author of *Reclaim Her Heart* and *Confidently Crowned*

"In a time when it is easy to be overwhelmed with all the bad and happiness seems to be a moving target, Brittany offers a better option. With practical steps and God's Truth, she teaches us how to embrace joy and hope."

—**Simi John,** speaker and author of *I Am Not: Break Free from Stereotypes & Become the Woman God Made You to Be*

"Brittany Estes is the coach, big sister, and best friend we all need. This book will make you laugh out loud and stand up and cheer. Equal parts powerful and personal, this book is the anthem of a generation of girls who speak truth over themselves, know their worth, and won't settle for less."

—**Grace Valentine,** best-selling author of *Am I Enough?*

"Brittany's heart for young women stepping into their identity in Christ is infectious, and this book is further equipping her mission that I love and champion so deeply!"

—**Ainsley Britian,** author of *Don't Date a Boo Boo Dude*

"The first time I ever heard a teaching from Brittany, I could tell God's light shined through her. She helps me to be a better person and someone I want to be. Brittany has changed my perspective on how I view the world. SO much love for her!"

—**Gracie A.,** 16 years old

"Brittany is a beacon of joy. I've never met anyone who represents the love of Jesus as much. She has the kindest and wisest heart, and she has led me in my faith with her amazing knowledge. Brittany is such a pure person; I look up to her so much and aspire to be like her!"

—**Carly F.,** 15 years old

"Brittany's words are encouraging and uplifting. They are something I look forward to each week. I have the joy of getting to meet with Brittany as a mentor weekly; she is one of the sweetest and most authentic people I've ever met. God works through her and her teaching. She leaves such an impact and is truly a light to those around her. I'm so excited to see what God does through her book *Glow Up!*"

—**Emily J.**, 16 years old

"Something about Brittany that you cannot miss is how Jesus radiates through her. She is someone I can come to about anything and never feel judged. She goes out of her way to make me feel loved and known. She is a prime example of a disciple of Jesus in how she spreads love to anyone she can. Brittany is someone I aspire to be like."

—**Scarlet R.**, 15 years old

"As a girl who's always struggled with my faith and has tried to find a good role model to lead me down a path with Christ, Brittany is just that. Her faith is unmatched. She stands strong in her beliefs, and she is genuinely one of the best people I have ever met. She takes time out of her day every Sunday to help a group of girls and me stay on a good path with the Lord. She is truly a blessing to be around, and I see God's light shining through her."

—**Emma G.**, 16 years old

"Brittany is one of my biggest role models. She has helped me so much in my journey with God, and I wouldn't be where I am today without her. Whenever I have a question about anything, I go to her, and she always has the answer. Jesus's light shines through her, and every time she teaches, I leave with more knowledge and understanding of God and his love for us. She is a true woman of God."

—**Shelby S.**, 16 years old

"Brittany is such an outgoing and encouraging person! She is easy to talk to, and my day is always brightened after talking with her. Brittany is an amazing person who helps others to grow closer to Jesus. She truly shines the light of him to all around her!"

—**Crosstyn R.**, 17 years old

glow up

A Teen's Guide to Flipping the Script

BRITTANY ESTES

LEAFWOOD

PUBLISHERS

an imprint of Abilene Christian University Press

GLOW UP
A Teen's Guide to Flipping the Script

LEAFWOOD
P U B L I S H E R S
an imprint of Abilene Christian University Press

Copyright © 2025 by Brittany Estes

ISBN 978-1-68426-362-2

Printed in the United States of America

Cataloging-in-Publication Data is on file at the Library of Congress, Washington, DC

Cover design and author photo by Allison Rodgers

Interior text design by Scribe Inc.

Leafwood Publishers is an imprint of Abilene Christian University Press
ACU Box 29138
Abilene, Texas 79699
1-877-816-4455
www.leafwoodpublishers.com

25 26 27 28 29 30 31 / 7 6 5 4 3 2 1

DEDICATION

Maggie:

May this book be a legacy in honor of your
life. Your time, though it was cut short, should
have been filled with so much potential and a
hopeful future. These are the things I wished
that I could have told you when you were a teen.
But now I hope they will be words to change
a generation. You are so loved and missed.

*Ethan, James, Poppy, Titus, Paisley,
Penelope, Pippa, and Asher:*

You are the reason I write. You are my biggest
calling and accomplishment. I'm so proud of you
and the beautifully unique individuals you are
becoming. God is awesome, and so are YOU!

GLOW UP DEDICATION

*For all of you listed here as well as the
ones who are not—this is for you.*

For our Girls!

For the girl who feels too much and
the one who feels not enough.
For the one who appears to have it all
and the one who sits alone at lunch.
For the athlete and the bookworm,
the loud and the shy.

This is your call.

You've allowed the world to dictate what
you do, how you look, and who to be.
You've let fear of these standards and perceived
shortcomings make you feel less than—
causing your light to dull.
But those days are over.

It's time.

You are uniquely created.
Beautifully woven from the inside out.
Your talents and skills call you to shine.
Embrace it. Be bold. Be you. GLOW!

When you shine, others can't help but follow.
Light the way so they too can find freedom.
Bring out the God-colors in this world.

Glow up, girl!

Poppy E.	Paisley E.	Penelope E.	Pippa E.
Eliana P.	Arabella P.	Hazel P.	Maddy Y.
Sophia B.	LillyAnn H.	Abigail D.	Adriana F.
Marley W.	Victoria T.	Grace K.	Lizzy Ann
Abbie M.	Ever R.	Gemma A.	Ava Grace B.
Brylynn L.	Abigail S.	Ellie N.	Avery S.
Charlee K.	Kiley S.	Addilyn S.	Lida L.
Kayla W.	Shelbi Lynn	Emily G.	Shelby G.
Molly B.	Ella S.	Lola L.	Vivian S.
Lucille S.	Isabel S.	Hayden S.	Rachel
Adriana	Karen P.	Angelina J.	Lena Marie H.
Blake G.	Lilah Rose P.	Dustie L.	Kallie H.
Kaylee M.	Addyson C.	Heidi M.	Kaylee S.
Taylor Rose R.	Ava D.	Olivia D.	Alexis T.
Jillian K.	Hope K.	Nahomy A.	Gigi A.
Gabby A.	Layla G.	Casey F.	Mallory N.
Elly L.	Abby L.	Brenleigh G.	Caroline S.
Taylor M.	Maci M.	Valentina H.	Ella G.
Emma G.	Shelby S.	Gracie A.	Emily J.
Scarlett R.	Carly F.	Julieann T.	Gigi R.
Ruby R.	Ashley L.	Crosstyn R.	Ava Grace D.
Emily L.	Briana M.	Elly	Ari
Oaklie B.	Kate N.	Molly J.	Caroline J.
Stella W.	Livie D.	Kayden	Ava T.
Mailey C.	Ella B.	Raegan L.	Natalie Anne
Layla C.	Faith S.	Hadley S.	Kinsleigh S.
Jocelyn	Aly V.	Ariel H.	Neely J.
	Kadence L.	Keian L.	

CONTENTS

introduction
THE SCRIPTS THAT DISTRACT US

Growing up I couldn't keep up with a diary. I always watched movies with girls furiously writing away in their beautifully decorated journals, using pens with feathered poufs on top. They'd lock the diaries up and shove them in a secret space, like under the bed or in the sock drawer, or if you were Lane Kim from *Gilmore Girls*, you'd hide your secrets under your bedroom floorboard. Classic. Side note: Never have I lived in a home where this could be possible; if I had, I might have been a better diary keeper. But it never seemed to work out for me.

Now, just because I never wrote in a journal doesn't mean that I didn't have any. Actually, I owned quite a few. Do you love a good journal or notebook? Oh goodness, I sure do. Even to this day I'll walk the notebook aisles in stores looking for ones that call out to me, begging me to bring them home. I'm pretty sure half the ones I own right now have nothing in them, but they feel too precious to fill with words—well, pointless words; they need real, deep, meaningful words.

I think this obsession started as a child. Each one was purchased or gifted to me in the hopes that it might spark my desire to write. All with no such luck. Some were decked out in sequins, others in bright colors, and a few leathered with a serious "writer's" feel to them. Without fail, I'd start out a day or two with grand plans to continue only to fade out by the end of the week. And then sometimes after writing my heart out, I'd hide my diary for safekeeping, only to realize I'd hidden it so well, I lost it. Clearly this whole ordeal just wasn't meant to be. My career as a writer would never be a thing.

Those thoughts sound rather comical now, because I wrote a book. And I don't mean the obvious one that you have nestled in between your fingers, but rather the one that came before this. That's the book I'm referring to. You see, I was on a journey to help a generation—the one right above you, in college and heading off into adulthood, to help them flip the script on the way they've been thinking. On the lies they believe. Because let's be real, these lies cause real harm. Lies ruin lives, break hearts, devastate an entire generation. Satan appeared to be winning this battle within their minds. But as this message from my first book reached the world, one thing became clear: I played it too small. What do I mean by that? This message wasn't and isn't just for that generation—quite the opposite. It's for everyone. Especially you.

People began to message me, sharing the impact of the book, but more times than not, they'd mention, "I wish I'd had this twenty years ago," or they'd say something similar. That's when you, my new teen bestie, came to mind. What would it look like for you to have the chance to flip your script right here, right now, before you're faced with the task of "twenty years of undoing" ahead of you? That's my hope. This is your chance to flip the script—a glow up, if you will. Because my desire is for you to take a deep breath and look over your story again with some new ideas in your head. As you read this book, let me walk alongside you so that you see how to *really* shine like God created you to.

But before we get started, let me ask you this:

Are there any mean statements playing in your head? Take a second to write them out.

_____

_____

_____

_____

_____

Here are a few I've listened to over the years:

You are too much.

People don't want to be your friend, because of YOU.

You'll never have a boyfriend.

You can never get anything right.

Maybe you resonated with a few of these statements. I'm sorry if so, but I want you to know that you're not alone. I've been there too. The good news is we can stop the statements in their tracks. You see, at the root of each of these statements is a lie, something harmful and untrue causing you to believe that you are less than God's best work. This is where I come in: your new pink-haired bestie, ready to tackle this mess with you. I'm well acquainted with your struggles. Honestly, they were mine too.

What if there is another way? What if your life doesn't have to be defined by what others say? Or even what you say to yourself over and over again? Or what social media mandates? What if I told you that beauty and life are yours to be found, all while being exactly who God created you to be? That your life could be different from the start?! What if you knew that freedom beckons you?

Freedom is possible. There is more for you, so much more. I hope you find hope in this book. I hope you mark up its pages, spill your drink on it, and wear it flat out, because once we're done with this book, you won't question how incredibly remarkable you are. Why? Because you'll learn something that will change the trajectory of your life. The truth is tucked in 2 Corinthians 10:5. It's simple but life-changing. The apostle Paul wrote, "We demolish arguments and every pretension that sets itself up against the knowledge of God, and we take captive every thought to make it obedient to Christ." The problem you've been facing? It is nothing but bad scripts containing negative, broken, lie-filled sentences that you hear in your head as you go to school, play, and go about your life.

These scripts are sidelining you, distracting you, and harming you. But they need not mess with you any longer. You will learn how to "take captive every thought" by flipping those internal scripts. I will show you how.

It's time to silence all the voices so you can hear the One who really matters. Whether you feel it or not, there is so much noise in your own head as you fight to grasp who you are, where you're going, and what you're worth. These negative scripts represent a lie, a distraction from the evil one. He can be so sneaky and persistent that he can have you all wrapped up in yourself to the point that you can't even see what's going on. You just feel lost, paralyzed, and defeated. You are too young to be feeling this way. This isn't the kind of life God hopes for you. But one thing is clear: Satan is predictable, and I have his number. Jesus reminds us in John 8:44, "He was a murderer from the beginning, not holding to the truth, for there is no truth in him. When he lies, he speaks his native language, for he is a liar and the father of lies."

Here is how we win. We're going to highlight some scripts that have broken you down or even have possibly flat-out shattered you. The great news is that you are never broken beyond repair. In fact, I want to show you how God plans to gently collect all your pieces and put them back together as you retrain your mind to think differently about your situation, God, and your world. Once you've learned how to flip your old script in a way that represents the truth of Scripture, you will emerge stronger than before. These are real-life script flips you can create to be made whole again. However, this journey is not easy or quick. Flipping negative scripts will take time and lots of work on your part. But you won't be doing it alone. I'm right here with you, cheering for you with a fresh new journal and bedazzled pen in hand. Do you have one too? These pages will give you moments to write, reflect, and respond. I hope you'll take the time to do so. If you need to make it a little fun (and really, who doesn't?), find a special pen to use just for this book. Then send me a picture on social media (Instagram is my favorite) with the hashtag #glowupbookpen so I can see how you tackled this message and encourage you. I can't wait to see! (And if you search the hashtag, you'll find a picture of mine as well!)

There will be freedom, trust me. I can speak to it because I've experienced it, not only in my life, but in the lives of many other people. But I don't want us to stop there; I need us to look around and see the girls who need us. They are counting on you to help them through it as well. You have the power to literally change this world—I know it, I can feel it. And your freedom will become contagious.

Are you ready for your glow up?

Let's discover your negative scripts and truly flip them.

one

OLD SCRIPT

I Am a Failure

I fail a lot. Seriously, your girl seems to mess things up and fall short often. When people ask what I'm good at, I jokingly answer, "Failing." And while it's good for a short laugh, most of the time I believe it. Let me explain.

In high school, I had a slight addiction . . . to tanning beds. Yes, I know now how silly that was, and I know all about the harm tanning beds can cause to your body. But as a high school sophomore, I believed firmly in my invincibility. This pasty white girl wanted a golden bronze color. So bring on the ultraviolet bed! Now the trend seems to be spray tans, but honestly that strikes a little more fear in me than the old-school beds. Why? Because my children joke of spray tans gone wrong and innocent bystanders leaving the session looking like "Oompa Loompas" boasting an orangey glow that could never appear natural. Apparently it's all too common with spray tans, and I'm not about to come out looking like I belong in Willy Wonka's chocolate factory. No sir, not gonna do it.

Even though I loved the sun beds, I will say that I was a stickler for wearing my goggles when I tanned. The worker at the tanning salon cautioned me about the effects of not wearing goggles and what it could do to my eyesight. I'm not always a rule follower, but in this case, this sister didn't need to be told twice; I wore goggles every time. Nothing could mess with my perfect twenty-twenty vision. Because of the goggles, I had amazing orange-and-white raccoon eyes. But at least I wasn't an "Oompa Loompa," am I right?!

Each day after school, I'd drive to the tanning salon and bake for twenty minutes. Shoot, even before I could drive, my grandma would take me after I got home off the bus. She'd drive me there and sit in the car smoking a cigarette while I went inside. (Yeah, Grandma was a character.) Oh, how I looked forward to those twenty minutes every day. Most of the time, I'd turn on the fan in my room, blast the music, and take a short little nap. Favorite part of my day. But one afternoon, things didn't go as planned. At some point in my heated nap session, my goggles slipped off my face, and my pasty white eyelids no longer looked white. Nope, they became like crusty lobsters. Yeah, it sounds as good as they looked.

School is tough, friends, especially high school, even in normal circumstances. *You* know what I'm talking about. But when your eyes are crusted and swollen and you're unable to wear makeup—that's just tragic. Or at least it felt that way to me. *Why did my parents make me go to school looking like this? Did they hate me?*

I knew I'd be a walking, crusted "joke target," and I'm not sure how you come back from that. Somehow, I persuaded the school administration to allow me to wear sunglasses until my eyelids healed. I think they just didn't want to hear me whine any longer. Either way, I sported my sassy 1950s-inspired leopard-print sunglasses for days. The situation went from being the worst to the coolest.

During my sunglasses phase, as I like to call it, we learned a new concept in geometry class. My teacher shut the lights off in the class as we followed along with her work on the projector. This dates me a bit—hello, 2001! But with the room dark and my sunglasses providing even more shade, I quickly fell asleep. In my mind, I still play out that day as if I were incognito and nobody even knew I slept. But who was I kidding? Everyone must've known. I was the ridiculous girl wearing sunglasses in the dark with her head on the desk, probably snoring. No secrecy. No mystery. That's when I missed the news about this particular geometric information: what we were just learning would appear on our semester test, and if we were to fail, we would be forced to take the class again.

Did I study for the test? No. I felt confident, aside from the crusty eyes. I always had. I could go in and take that test and pass with flying colors. Not this time. I didn't just fail; I failed miserably. There I sat, in a group of class clowns, troublemakers, and other slacker kids pulled into a special class to retake the semester. It was so embarrassing and all my fault. Lack of effort and desire to try proved to be my downfall. Hidden behind my sunglasses, I chose to nap and not pay attention, and because of that, I faced the consequences.

The whole story is a joke in my family. "Brittany's so good at math that she took Geometry *twice*." Or "You would know, you took the class twice!" Cue the laughter. It's all said to tease, and shoot, sometimes I'm the one leading the charge. But if I'm honest with you, that script stings. Those words hurt then and still hurt now. It's hard to believe in yourself, your dreams, and your abilities when you think about how you've failed. The script plays like a broken record. *You can't do this; you're too lazy. Remember that one time you failed here? That's all you're good at.* More times than I'd like to admit, I believe the script as truth. I accept defeat before I even try, all because of a careless sentence thrown my way. Remember, "The tongue has the power of life and death, and those who love it will eat its fruit" (Prov. 18:21).

It doesn't have to be a big or scary event, but the seed of failure can be planted at any moment. And before you know it, it's grown into a giant tree with deep roots, blocking you from seeing the truth or moving forward in your future. Instead, it causes you to freeze and hide behind it. That's the power of a negative script.

My daughter Paisley was on the track team in seventh grade. Now, if you're familiar with track, you know that everyone likes to run the short distances and events. Everyone loves the speed and glory that come with these races. Not many even entertain the idea of the longest distance—two miles. For most of Paisley's first season, the team didn't have anyone running that race. That was until the coach caught wind of how my girl ran a mile with me every day. Without her knowledge, he signed her up for the two-mile race, just to get her feet in the door and a chance to practice. Really, he believed she would be more than capable to compete at that distance, but he only wanted her to test it out in this race. Panic and fear set in as she worried that she wouldn't be able to finish, that she would look like a fool in front of all the onlookers, and ultimately that she'd fail.

Because she was so nervous, the coach allowed me to jump on the field with the other coaches to cheer and encourage her. I reminded Paisley of what the coach said: "I don't care if you finish last; that's not the goal. Just don't stop and don't walk." She replied, "I know, I just don't want to get lapped." No sooner did the words leave her mouth than they announced that the boys and girls would race at the same time. The odds were definitely not in her favor now. Even though the boys would be ranked separately from the girls, I knew Paisley would see them lapping her as a defeat.

The gun went off, and within a couple of laps, the boys passed her. I could see the defeat in her eyes as tears welled up, and I knew she wanted to quit. That's when I went up beside her and started running the inside grassy loop alongside her. "Paisley, you're doing the hard work. The work nobody else wants to do. See those people in the stands? They took the easy way out, but you're still here." With each lap she slowed and begged to stop because she was so embarrassed. I knew in my heart she could finish, but according to her standards, she had already failed. "Remember, your goal is to finish last; that's great! The only rules are don't stop and don't walk.

You can do this." As I ran with her cheering, I started to cry with Paisley, because I knew she was doing the hard thing. The thing that she thought she was messing up at. The thing that she wanted to quit, but she didn't.

When Paisley finally crossed the finish line, her team jumped up and roared with cheers, chanting her name. But she crumpled to the ground deflated. Lap after lap she believed she let her team, her family, and herself down. She was a failure and an embarrassment. My heart broke, because where she saw failure, I beamed with pride over her determination and courage. She showed up for something she had never done, she fought valiantly through each lap, and she never quit. She was a warrior. Even though we cheered loudly every encouragement known to man, in the quiet of her mind, all she heard was *You're a failure. Everyone is laughing at you. You should be embarrassed.*

It's the small, simple scripts that stick the longest. They're sneaky like that, and the longer they have the freedom to run your heart and mind, the harder they are to correct. Because they are short and sly, you don't even realize there's a problem until you see how they've spread through your entire life and have caused you to question every choice, mistake, or direction—to wonder if current struggles are a reflection of past failings, God's punishments, or your entire worth. You start to believe that life would be easier if you were good enough, if you made all the right choices, if you never let people down. Can you relate? I would bet that I'm not alone in these thoughts. Remember, I'm good at failing. We forget this simple statement: "There is no one righteous, not even one" (Rom. 3:10).

A few years back, I found myself on a stage while helping host a children's ministry event with my husband, Sam. That particular night, the church was packed with people of all ages. It was such a fun sight to behold. At the end of the event, we brought up our favorite dancing third grader, and I challenged him to a dance-off.

My plan was to make the crowd laugh; I'm pretty good at that, so that wouldn't prove too hard. That's when our little third-grade buddy started to breakdance. *Say what? It's fine, I'm fine, everything's fine. This kid is going down*, I thought. He busted a few moves that I couldn't name even if I tried, so I answered back with some hilarious attempts of my own. That's when I decided to get serious. After his next series of ridiculously skilled stunts, I dropped down trying to land a one-handed handstand trick. The crowd would jump to their feet in an uproar while cheering me on, because who doesn't get excited seeing a thirty-year-old woman breakdance? But things didn't go as planned. When I tried to stick the move, my hand gave out, and I collapsed onto the floor. Somewhere between the adrenaline rush of excitement and the horror of the fall, I heard a pop. *Shoot. This can't be good.* But as a trained theater actor, I hopped up, shook my hand, and continued on with the show. The reality hit the moment I stepped off the stage. My thumb throbbed.

After a few days of denial and a giant black-and-blue hand, we realized that this might be a big deal. A trip to the orthopedist confirmed that it was worse than we imagined. Not only did I break my thumb, but a piece of bone that was attached to the muscle became detached, and I had another tear straight down the top of my thumb. All of that would result in a surgery, a gnarly scar, three casts, and four months of rehab. Still to this day, I struggle to open containers or grip things with that thumb for extended periods of time.

Every time people ask what happened to me, I laugh and say that I broke my thumb while breakdancing. Because obviously that's the answer you expect from a sane, grown adult. What an unexpected story: the time I failed and did so massively in front of a large crowd of people.

The pain of failure is real and, in my case, costly. Often, that negative script causes me to pause for fear of failing all over again. Who wants to take chances when the cost of failing can be so great?

Maybe that's why we've stopped taking risks, moving forward, and contemplating our purpose. We think, "Just play it safe."

I'm a life coach, did you know that? Specifically, I'm an inner dialogue coach, helping women and teens discover the lies they believe and replace them with truth. Not many things excite me more than seeing the excitement that comes when my client finds freedom in an area they were stuck in. I've noticed with coaching teens that there seems to be one big common obstacle they face: the fear of failure. If it's not perfect or they won't succeed, they can't seem to bring themselves to try or to take a step. Recently, I put out a poll on social media to see what teenagers would identify as their biggest struggle or roadblock for their future. Wouldn't you know it, over 90 percent of them answered back with some sort of "fear of failure." They didn't want to fail at school, in their friendships, as a child, and so on. You name it, they worried they would unavoidably fail at it. Many were too afraid to share their God-given dreams and talents for fear of failing at those too. There is something worse than failure, and that's the fear of failure, which can paralyze and even kill you. I've seen it happen many times. It will do more harm, kill more dreams, and ruin more lives than failure ever will.

Why do we let fear rule us? Could it be our past failures? Are we still listening to old scripts about them? Are we letting them rule us from years past?

I met Megan through a friendship with her mother. She was a beautiful, fun, and bright girl—until she found herself trapped in the stress and chaos of high school. One evening I sat down to chat with her and see how life and school were going when I realized there was a big issue. Megan felt stuck and pressured to be perfect. Honestly, she isn't the only teen girl I've talked to who feels this. I bet you do too, right!? Her assignments piled up, misunderstandings with friends weighed on her, and the idea that she could never measure up left her crippled. Megan's grades plummeted; she began to isolate herself and would hide in her bedroom at home. What happened? What shifted for her? A few months prior, Megan had been assigned a project for her science class. She spent hours researching, planning, and building the perfect ecosystem. Truly it looked incredible. I know, because she showed me a picture. Pride beamed from her smile and confidence through her eyes as she walked into class to turn in her work. She knew deep in her heart she'd get a perfect score, maybe even bonus points for her creativity, but what she saw a few weeks later she was not prepared for. Megan's grade: a low D. Apparently in all of the designing and building process, she missed one step. This one step cost her grade quite a bit. But to make matters worse, the teacher wrote, "Great project, but maybe if you spent time reading the guidelines and less on building this structure, you'd have a better grade." Ouch. The words crushed Megan. And in that moment, she shut down. "If I'm going to mess up, I might as well just not even try." She feared making a mistake and decided she wouldn't fail like that again. This fear of failure left her frozen and unable to make any moves forward. Then through that decision, she began to admit defeat before even trying anything new, causing her to fail right from the beginning. Megan found herself in a vicious cycle. Each time Megan failed, she felt even worse about herself, which would in turn remind her of how she wasn't perfect—she couldn't do things right, and then she would decide not to try and to shut down, because even if she did, she'd fail. And this caused her to spiral, sinking lower and lower, feeling even more overwhelmed with and sad about her life.

Yes, there is pain in failure. It can cut deep, leaving scars and reminders like a breakdancing move gone wrong. It can haunt you with your past decisions or current circumstances—a part of your story that won't let go and can't be forgotten. Rather than risk feeling this again, we run and hide, never moving forward while our negative script screams in our head, *Do you see how you've messed up? Nothing good could ever come of you again. You're a failure.*

But I know this is true: we all mess up. We all make mistakes—that's the human condition. But God promised the prophet something deeply encouraging. Just as Isaiah wanted to throw in the towel as his nation was heading toward imminent exile, God said this: "Don't be afraid, for I am with you. Don't be discouraged, for I am your God. I will strengthen you and help you. I will hold you up with my victorious right hand" (Isa. 41:10 NLT). This is true for you as well. God is with you. He will strengthen you—even when you fail.

- Have you ever felt like you've failed? What happened? How did it feel?

- Has fear ever stopped you from taking a step? Maybe with friends, in school, at church, or in sports?

- Let's write down the negative scripts that come to mind when we think about failure and the stories we wrote above.

Don't be afraid,
for I am with you.
Don't be discouraged,
for I am your God.
I will strengthen you
and help you.
I will hold you up
with my victorious
right hand.

—

ISA. 41:10 NLT

two

NEW SCRIPT

I Am Not a Failure

When I was a teen, I wanted to become famous. Shocker, I know. But I just knew that I'd be one of those overnight success stories, a girl of greatness discovered singing in her local church or acting on stage at her high school. Never mind the odds of this happening, I believed that I'd be the one to defy the odds, because I was something special with one-of-a-kind talent. To be honest, I think this seems to be the teenage condition. We believe all things are possible as a child; we grow up watching movies where magic happens, people can fly, and the possibilities are limitless. Fun fact, as a middle schooler, a girl around my age rose to fame with her debut album, . . . *Baby One More Time.* Her name: Britney Spears. Why does this matter? Because of my name before I got married—Brittany Sears. Yes, I grew up with people interchanging my name with hers. We were practically the same person with two very different lives. Her life was what my dreams were made of, and I just needed us to be besties.

With both excitement and full belief in one day making it big and finally meeting Britney Spears, I joined any and all opportunities available to me for theater and choir. I remember one time, in our church's youth choir, that I landed a solo for a song we planned to sing a few weeks later. Yeah, that was a thing back in my day, youth group choirs. If you need a reference, watch the movie *Sister Act 2*; we were the cool kids singing "Oh Happy Day" to an innocent, quiet crowd in the church auditorium, and yet, we were something special.

Each week at practice we rehearsed the number with my part, and I grew eager to sing in front of the crowd. But at one particular practice the girl next to me heard my voice and leaned over after we finished: "You were flat. Man, I can't even do that." Oh my goodness, I must be good if she can't even be flat like I am, I thought. Little did I know at the time, being "flat" while singing isn't a positive thing. In case you are naive like me, if someone tells you that you're singing flat, they mean that you are singing a note lower in pitch than the note intended. When I thought the girl had complimented my stellar skills, she definitely had not.

To make matters worse, the night we sang in front of the church, I embarrassed myself completely. We all staggered to our spots, strategically poised and seated on the steps of the stage like a boy band cover photo; the music began to play. In one of the breaks before my solo, there was an instrumental interlude. I had performed this many times before in the weeks prior, but for some reason that night I messed up counting myself in. Yep, I began singing too soon. Some of the group looked up at me with a look that screamed, "NOT YET, SHUT UP!" But instead of heeding their glares, I chose a different path. One that if I were in the same situation today, I might rethink. Instead of going silent, I continued to sing my heart out through the whole thing, thinking the crowd wouldn't know. Quitting would be me admitting defeat. So I pressed on.

Was it pretty? Oh heck no. Actually, it was painfully embarrassing. To this day I will tell people that I'm not a singer because I remember the horror of it all. I am *not* the world's best singer, and I am happy to let others stand in the spotlight on that front. But the thing I remember most? The fact that I never quit . . . well, that night I never quit.

It can be easy to quit when you mess up. To throw in the towel, hide your head in the sand, and never come out again. The sinking feeling of failure is real. I can speak to moments when that script was the only one I could hear, and the cry blared so loud, I doubted my worth and everything I ever believed. Like my career as a famous pop star, really just a silly thing, the failing moment and rejection spoke so loudly and scared me deeply. Do you also know that feeling? I know I'm not alone in this. Talking with teens all the time, I hear they are affected by past failures, big and small. Those shortcomings, mistakes, or failures have broken them. They have made them fragile shells of the girls God created them to be. Yes, I know that feeling. I've listened to that script, and I've been crushed by it before. Just like you.

So here I sit, writing this book to you, with words I needed to hear and you do too. Truth be told, this message was a fight to get to your hands. Through the journey of writing, I've faced many rejections, nos, and "you're flat" moments. The sting of each one brought me back to moments of previous failure and mess-ups. But unlike my singing career, I haven't quit. I could have let the "no/failure" scripts ring louder in my ears than the urgency and passion God has given me for you. But I've done that before, you know. Here's the deal: what I found, hidden in the rejection and overshadowed by the failure, was the fact that I was the one who was suffering. I wanted to try something different with this book and for you. What did I have to lose? This time the *no* would allow me to be braver, fear less about what others' reactions or my setbacks might be, and focus on the calling in front of me. That calling is you, and I want you to be brave with me. Maybe you don't believe there can be a future or hope outside of your current reality. *(I'm so sorry if this is you; I wish that I could reach through this book and hug you so tight.)*

Maybe you're thinking, *That's great, Brittany, but I don't think it will work for me. My failure wasn't a silly phone call, a bad grade, or even the fear of something scary. No, I really messed up my life. I found out I was pregnant, got expelled from school, or was caught trying drugs.*

OK, but what if I told you that I know a guy—you know, in my best mobster shrug, lips curled, raspy whisper kind of way. Because I do. I know a guy named David who messed up big-time. Maybe you've read about him in the Bible.

King David was a man respected and loved by many. He had almost everything he could ever want. But here's the problem: he wanted a married woman. Almost as if it were a plot twist in a romance movie, the woman ended up pregnant. David messed up, and in a panic, he scrambled to cover up what he had done: "David wrote a letter to Joab and gave it to Uriah to deliver. The letter instructed Joab, 'Station Uriah on the front lines where the battle is the fiercest. Then pull back so that he will be killed'" (2 Sam. 11:14–15 NLT).

I once walked into my kitchen to see my two-year-old and my entire kitchen floor covered in powdered sugar—like Santa had dropped the North Pole off right in my house. As I looked at my little man, eyelids heavy from the weight of the white powder, chest covered, wearing only a diaper, clearly trying to mask the mess behind him, I asked Ethan what happened, to which he replied, "Nothing." That "nothing" looked like a whole lot of something that I was going to have to clean up.

That too was King David, but on a much larger scale. He was stuck in his mistake, covered in powder, and trying to hide it. But instead of owning up, he had the woman's husband killed. Just like my toddler, he thought nobody would ever know. But God knew, and he sent a messenger to tell David. Once David realized the jig was up and the weight of what he had done hit him, he was crushed. This man, once known for slaying giants and killing vicious animals, crumbled at his great failure: "Then David confessed to Nathan, 'I have sinned against the LORD.' Nathan replied, 'Yes, but the LORD has forgiven you, and you won't die for this sin'" (2 Sam. 12:13 NLT).

Have you found yourself crushed by the weight of your failures, especially the ones that seem so earthshaking and huge? Me too. But here's what I need you to see. David didn't just hang up his robe, call it a day, and lie around waiting to die. No, he owned his failures, cried out to God, and begged him to make things right in his heart again, to clean up the powdered sugar mess like I had to for Ethan: "God, make a fresh start in me. . . . Don't throw me out with the trash, or fail to breathe holiness in me. Bring me back from gray exile, put a fresh wind in my sails!" (Ps. 51:10–12 *The Message*).

David's sin and cover-up didn't define his entire life. His actions did have severe consequences (see 2 Sam. 12:10–12 for the graphic repercussions), but as we see in Scripture, we know David for so much more. In fact, he's known for being a man after God's own heart. That's what we remember him for. And can I tell you something? You have the chance to start afresh too, my friend. The road won't be easy, there may be consequences, and Satan will try to remind you of your failures at every step forward. But you can get back up, and your past doesn't have to define you. If we follow Jesus, we know that sin and our old lives no longer control us; we are new people. Like 2 Corinthians 5:17 says, "This means that anyone who belongs to Christ has become a new person. The old life is gone; a new life has begun!" (NLT). It's not just the old life that's gone; so is the weight of our negative scripts.

We have a goldendoodle named Walt, and he is the cutest, most precious dog in the world. Yes, I know you thought that title belonged to your pup. Sorry to disappoint you, but it does not. Walt is just the best. He and I love to go on runs together. He looks forward to them every day. I cannot come out of my bedroom dressed in workout clothes without him attacking me, eager to head out for a run. He knocks me over as I stretch, weaving in and out around my body as it bends like a pretzel. It's quite comical. But once we finally head out the door on our run, he is straight business. Many times, that guy pulls me along for *his* run. I've been known to clock a 4:40 mile with Walt at the helm.

Without fail, though, every time we go on our runs, Walt can be counted on to poop. He is not sorry to stop, drop, and relieve himself no matter where we are or who is around. This is just a fact of life for him. Is it annoying to stop midstride to allow him to handle his business? Yes. Does it stink? Yes. Do I wish I didn't have to deal with the aftermath? Yes. But just because the action Walt engages in every run is "crap," I'm not going to label him a "crapper." *Hey friends, have you met my little crapper?* No, he is so much more than that. His worth isn't defined by that one act. Instead, when I think of Walt, I think of my best friend, my cuddle partner, and a straight-up joy to be around.

The same is true with failure. Failing is an action and a stinky one at that. But somehow, somewhere, we have adopted the term *failure* to go along with it. *Failure* is a label of shame, one we use to devalue our lives, abilities, and worth. *Hi, my name is Brittany, and I'm a failure.* That one word packs together all our shortcomings, mess-ups, inadequacies, and crap. It's a weight we seem to own, cling to, and carry.

But what if we don't have to?

Sister, if I were face-to-face with you right now, I'd grab your shoulders, lock eyes with you, and preach truth to your heart. I'm sorry that you have listened to a failure script for so long. I'm sorry that you feel your worth is defined by your abilities to succeed or please others. I'm sorry that you find yourself hidden in rejection and overshadowed by failure.

Here's what I need you to know. You are not a failure, and you are worth far more than you give yourself credit for. I know, because I've seen it played out in my life and the lives of many teens I've had the pleasure of meeting.

I know that sometimes our minds are the most brutal places to be. There we create scripts like *You'll always mess up. You'll never succeed. You deserve this setback.* If we stay with these negative scripts, we are apt to live them. The author of Proverbs reminds us how important our hearts are: "Guard your heart above all else, for it determines the course of your life" (Prov. 4:23 NLT).

The scripts rolling around in our heads can tear us down and tell us who we are and what we aren't. It can make us feel defeated, overwhelmed, insecure, and worthless. Before we know it, the loop playing over and over sends us into a toxic spiral. Consider the following negative scripts. Perhaps you relate? And then choose the positive scripts based on the Bible that will help you retrain your mind toward the freedom and joy Jesus has for you.

- Old script: *I will never amount to anything.* New script: *Because of what Jesus did for me, I have a brand-new life* (2 Cor. 5:17).

- Old script: *I deserve this struggle.* New script: *God promises to work all things out for my good and his glory* (Rom. 8:28).

- Old script: *All I do is mess up.* New script: *God's grace is all I need because God's power works best in my weaknesses* (2 Cor. 12:9).

- Old script: *I am too afraid.* New script: *God has not given me a spirit of fear but one of power, love, and sound mind* (2 Tim. 1:7).

⋆ًⵌًⵌ It's Time for Your Glow Up!

What are some scripts you need to flip? Below, write them out and ask God to help you flip them. You can also look through your Bible, maybe google verses dealing with this topic, or even ask trusted friends, family, or leaders to help you.

Old Script: _____

New Script: _____

Old Script: _____

New Script: _____

Old Script: _____

New Script: _____

You are not merely the sum of your thoughts. You *can* overcome the familiar scripts you have wrongly believed as truth. John promises us, "You, dear children, are from God and have overcome them, because the one who is in you is greater than the one who is in the world" (1 John 4:4). With the strength of the Holy Spirit who resides in you, you can rewrite the script you listen to and can release the ideals of perfection. You are going to mess up, make mistakes, and get things wrong. But this does not make you a failure. This makes you a human. You are worth far too much to believe anything less.

You have a chance; you have a future. Dispel the negative scripts trying to take root in your heart. Believe that God will use all this for your good and his glory. And keep moving forward. God is not done, and Paul reminds us of this in Philippians 1:6: "And I am certain that God, who began the good work within you, will continue his work until it is finally finished on the day when Christ Jesus returns" (NLT). Next are some practical ways to transform your scripts.

♛ Find the Triggers

Notice when your thoughts start bringing you down. What's going on when this happens? Who's around you? Pinpoint the harmful words, and write out your negative script. This will help you determine the root cause lurking beneath—something every bad thought has. Most of the time, your negative script is buried deep in a lie you are believing. But you can't work to change the script unless you first call out the root lie and dialogue beneath it all.

- Do any lies come to mind? It helps to get them out of your head; don't leave them stuck inside. Write them out.

♛ Finish the Statement

Conclude your negative script with the words "in Jesus's name." If the statement you're believing doesn't sound right when it's followed by "in Jesus's name," then it probably isn't true. (For example: *Man, I am so dumb . . . in Jesus's name.*) It is amazing how quickly you can pick out lies by using this tool. The words spoken about you partnered with the name of Jesus should never make you feel broken and filled with shame. They should make you feel seen and loved.

Try this out: write one phrase that sounds correct and another with a negative script.

Negative statement:

_____ _____, in Jesus's name.

Truth statement:

_____, in Jesus's name.

Do you hear the difference? I hope so. In the future, before you agree with a thought in your head or a statement someone else says about you, try to use this phrase. You don't have to agree with or believe everything, and it helps to know how/where to measure it up against.

 Seek Truth

Find truth to replace the lie. My favorite thing to do is create a list of scriptures that I can go to when my mind starts to spiral. Grab a small index card–size spiral notebook, and write down the negative script you struggle with. As you pray and find scriptures that combat your old script, write them down. A small notebook is perfect to throw in your purse/backpack or keep in your room. It's the perfect reminder and way to tangibly flip your script. Nothing fights fear, doubt, worthlessness, or overwhelm like the Word of God! Read your scripture list out loud to yourself because there's power in those words. I've been known to paste verses on my mirror, in my car, and even on the wall in front of my toilet. It's a good way to keep busy. Fun fact: I do this for my kids as well. On big state testing days for them, I write affirmations, verses, and so on on their arms with a Sharpie. It's encouragement for them when they need it most.

Speak Up

Talk to safe people. This may include a counselor, pastor, family, or friend. Find someone you trust who can call out these negative scripts and help you find truth. No good comes from battling lies in silence. If you don't have a safe person, call me. I will be that person for you. I'm not kidding. My number is posted in the back of this book; I'm only a phone call or text away. You are not alone, you will never be alone, and if you can't see past the fear, call me. Or shoot, if you want to discuss your love of coffee and Mexican food, you can call me about that too. Because I always want to talk.

- Do you have safe people in your life? If so, write them below. I want to encourage you to let them know that they are a safe person for you.

_____

_____

_____

_____

- If you're still looking for safe people, write down the names of a few people who could be this for you. Watch them and see how they make you feel, then pray about it. Maybe God has people right in front of you and you don't realize it.

_____

_____

_____

_____

Friends, our minds are battlefields. Some days will feel like winning, and others will look a lot like surviving. But one thing is certain: if you are a follower of Christ, the battle is already won. Suit up and claim that victory because, sister, according to the Word of God, you are *not* a failure.

glow up
DECLARATION

You are not a failure.

No mess-up, mistake,

or shortcoming can make you

any less loved.

You've been given grace

for this day and every day in the future.

You don't have to be perfect;

you get to try.

This is the best gift you've been given.

You are loved by God

no matter what.

Today, show up and try;

this is the beauty of

being human.

Here's something you need to know about me: I'm a big kid. It's true. While the facts are that I'm a wife, I'm a mom to eight kids, and I have a busy full-time job, the truth is that I'm always down for a party. Where's the fun?!

When paying bills, cleaning the house, or even doing other boring tasks, you'll find me looking for ways to make them more exciting. Whether it's pretending I'm on a daytime talk show, with a hair brush in one hand, explaining my techniques as I wipe down the bathroom mirror with the other; setting timers to see if I can beat the clock when completing my tasks; or probably my favorite way to make things more exciting—turning things into a game or competition. Are you competitive? My family sure is.

One evening after dinner, we asked our youngest kid to pick up some items left scattered across the floor downstairs. This did not excite him; in fact, he began moving slowly in protest, dragging his feet across the floor, his back slumped, as he bent over to pick up a discarded sock. For some reason we have socks *all over the house.* My children walk in the door, throw them off their feet, and leave them wherever they land. Anyway, very quickly I realized this simple chore would take an eternity if I let said child continue at his current pace. That's when an idea hit me. We'd turn it into a game. With my phone at the ready, I timed how quickly he could take the items up and down the stairs, placing them in their proper locations. It didn't take long for my son to laugh with excitement as he raced the clock trying to finish. That kid ramped up his speed, so much so that everyone in the house took notice. And in true Estes fashion, we created a challenge for the whole family—a race to see who could run up then walk down the stairs fifteen times in a row the fastest. In the end, I was not the winner, but the entire family had a blast as we laughed with and cheered for one another. Definitely a fun yet exhausting memory for sure.

This is my point. I love having fun. A few years ago, our student ministry asked me to attend their summer camp as a leader. Before I could even think twice about it, they mentioned the camp would take place at the beach. Need I say anymore? Of course, I blurted out a *yes!* before they had the chance to finish the sales pitch. The week of camp lived up to all the hype. Our days were spent with exciting Rec Team challenges (remember, I'm very competitive), restful afternoons at the beach, and incredible nights of worship and teaching. At the end of each night, the leaders would circle up with their groups and discuss what they had just heard in the big group. This particular night, when I sat with my group of girls, we got on the topic of "worth." As the conversation lulled, and the candy placed in the middle of the circle no longer enticed them to share, I asked one question. Truthfully, I expected there to be awkward silence, crickets, and darting of the eyes until someone reluctantly gave an answer. But what happened surprised me. Not even a second after asking the question, there was a unanimous *no* from everyone in the group. Do you want to know what the question was? "Do you see yourself as God sees you?" The answer was no. No. And this wasn't a speedy reply to move the conversation along; I could see the truth of the word written all over their faces. A mix of sadness and desperation, one that still breaks my heart to this day. But the more I work with teenagers, the more I understand that this answer isn't an isolated case. Many feel the same way. Now let me ask you this:

Do you see yourself as God sees you?

_____

_____

_____

_____

What do you see when you think of yourself?

_____

_____

_____

_____

As the girls opened up, sharing why they said no, it became clear that they were measuring their lives against their mistakes, what they weren't, what they wished they were, and how they could never be good enough. One sweet teenager, Gina, went on to share that she worked hard to make the best grades and be one of the fastest on the track team. If she didn't, she feared her parents wouldn't be proud of her or her friends might make fun of her. The weight of this pressure brought tears to her eyes as she hugged her knees, tucked tight into her chest. Without any warning, I could feel myself begin to choke back tears. I understood her words because I had felt them to my core. Why is it that we as girls never feel like we're enough? And why is it that we only want to be enough? What if we were meant for more than that?

On the floor, staring at the precious faces around me, I so desperately wanted them to believe that they were worthy, worthy enough for God to love. Most knew he loved them but struggled to fully accept the idea that he saw value in who they were individually.

Somewhere along the line, the truth of who God created each of them to be and what he thought of them became twisted. Shame entered the picture, and they felt that their worth was diminished. Yes, they made mistakes. No, they weren't perfect. No, they couldn't measure up to a God who was. But here's the cool thing: God knew they couldn't, and in his kindness, he called them worthy. They were worth bridging the gap and making a way for them to be his forever. These girls needed a glow up.

Maybe you have felt like this too: that sinking feeling in the pit of your stomach when you thought you just didn't measure up. Have there been moments when you've never been surer of your completely worthless existence? These could be fleeting thoughts or ones that plague your mind daily. Either way, you're not alone.

I come across teenagers and women—and, shoot, men—all the time who question their value and worth. Whether I'm on a stage teaching hundreds of teenagers about their purpose or coaching them one-on-one, this seems to be a topic we can't avoid. It's the ultimate negative script. Because if you believe you have no value and no worth and that you'll never measure up, the enemy doesn't have to distract you any other way. Here's the problem—we have forgotten who we are. It's like we're at the price-check station at Target, scanning ourselves over and over again and hoping the results will make us whole. But for some reason or another, the price we see never satisfies us. Why is that? Listen, those stations are super handy, and I love a good sale (can I get an amen?). In fact, I pride myself on scoring the best deals for my holiday shopping. But despite popular belief, Target doesn't have all the answers. Target is not where you shop to understand and know your worth. No, that answer can't be found in the world; it's discovered in God's Word. Paul wrote to the Romans, telling them about how to truly learn to flip their negative script: "Don't copy the behavior and customs of this world, but let God transform you into a new person by changing the way you think. Then you will learn to know God's will for you, which is good and pleasing and perfect" (Rom. 12:2 NLT).

When I was younger, I had the biggest crush on teen heartthrob Heath Ledger. You probably don't know who I'm talking about, and that is one of life's greatest tragedies, this I know. So do yourself a favor and google him. Just know that he was the cutest. Like make-grown-women-swoon kind of cute. He had dark, shaggy hair; a perfect Australian accent; and a smile that could melt you like a popsicle in the July Texas heat. So smitten by Heath, I made it my mission to watch all the movies he starred in. It became a sport to me. Then I proceeded to dream about the day when we would actually meet and he would inevitably fall in love with me. *Mrs. Brittany Ledger*, I could see it now. Of course, it was a one-in-a-million chance, but I remembered the words of Lloyd from *Dumb and Dumber*: "So you're saying there's a chance!"[1] To me, this seemed possible. When the movie *A Knight's Tale* opened in theaters, I claimed a front-row seat. It was cinematic perfection on a screen and solidified my desire to become Heath's bride.

In case you've been deprived of this rom-com genius, let me break it down for you. A peasant boy named William dreams of one day becoming a great knight. He hopes to "change the stars" and create a different future for himself. I can't fault him; I've often wished I could change my stars as well. Thankfully, I'm not stuck in medieval times and desperate for food after the sudden passing of my master. That's when he and his fellow servant buddies come up with a plan. They are going to fake William's royal lineage so he can compete in tournaments to earn money, fame, and a chance to be a real knight. As I'm sure you know, like any good romance movie, there is a beautiful girl that catches the attention of William. Now he wants not only to win for fame but also to win her over. It's not long before William's winning streak at these medieval tournaments catches up to him. All this attention isn't the best for a man who isn't really a knight but an impostor. Adhemar, our villain and a man whose ego is so big, he'd be the guy caught sweet-talking his own reflection, feels threatened by the accomplishments of William. To make matters worse, he too wants the love and affection of William's girl.

William and Adhemar find themselves in an intense jousting match against each other, a real David and Goliath moment—who will come out triumphant? Each man lines up at the start, seated on his horse, lance in hand, with the ultimate goal to defeat the other. As the flag rises and the men begin to charge, the crowd cheers and waits with great anticipation. The same could be said for me, with my bowl of popcorn, Coke in hand, and a stomach full of anxiety. *Would William beat his enemy?!* He had to win; I just knew it. The crowded theater all watched as the men charged on their horses, the lances smashed against each other, and wood splintered in all directions. Horror overtook our faces as William flew off his horse and crashed to the ground. Our hopes sank with William's defeat. That's when Adhemar walked over to his opponent, who was still lying on the ground, and said, "You have been weighed, you have been measured, and you have been found wanting."[2] William, wishing for a better future, tries to change his stars, but he comes up short. Adhemar is all too eager to remind him of that fact.

Even to this day, I can remember that quote. Words spoken in a theater by fictional characters, meant for our entertainment, found a place in my heart. When I least expected it, they resurfaced and reminded me of what I was and, more importantly, what I wasn't. I was reminded of when I didn't make the team; when my friends had boyfriends but no guy wanted me, which led me to believe I was ugly; when I didn't meet others' expectations; when pictures on social media reminded me of parties I wasn't invited to and outings I didn't make the cut for; when others appeared incredibly successful and the only thing I successfully did was hear the word *no.*

I thought about that movie and those words as I sat down for my first counseling session. *(I'm sharing this with you because I think you may know how I feel, but also, I want you to see that it's normal and very OK to see a counselor. There are many great professionals who can help you when you find yourself struggling, sad, or needing help. In fact, if you ever need a coach, call or text me.)* On a teal, L-shaped sectional full of fun pillows, I had no idea where to sit. *Do I go to the end? Maybe I should sit in the middle? Do I lean all the way back? Curl up like I'm going to watch a movie? And why are there so many pillows?* The inner corner was where I settled, with my elbows resting on my knees as I leaned forward, prepped for what was to come. Like a football player, I was poised for the snap. That was me, unsure of the opponent's plan but listening for the quarterback's signal.

Lucy was my counselor. She was a tall, beautiful blonde who had a flair for the bohemian and a perfectly eclectic taste that seamlessly reflected throughout her office space. Her face knew no other expression than to smile, and her eyes assured me that she really saw me and loved who I was, right in that moment. The thing I loved about Lucy was her quiet confidence. Her presence calmed my racing heart. You need people in your life who make you feel seen, and Lucy saw me. I mean, technically, I paid her to do that, but who's splitting hairs?

The first time I sat in her office, I blurted out that I wasn't upset to be there. Something I thought she should know, even though counseling hadn't been *my* choice. Instead, the decision found me as a mandate from my job at the time after a crazy summer where burnout became my reality. I had nothing against counseling and could benefit from time with her, but the circumstances around my arrival to that teal couch were less than ideal. Either way, I nervously clutched onto a bright orange fuzzy pillow and cracked a joke. Because that's what I do when things get too heavy. Yes, you can always trust me to come in clutch with a lighthearted comment to break the tension and make you laugh.

While I can usher in the fun like no one else, I also try to avoid pain. Who likes pain, anyway? That's why when things get too hard, heavy, or deep, I'll quickly rush in with a joke or funny story. If you ask me, it's a gift. Until it's not.

Lucy had her work cut out for her. I assured her that I was ready for all that therapy had to offer. *Fix this hot-mess girl up.* Clearly people *did* think I was a hot mess, or they wouldn't have asked me to go to therapy, so in my mind, there was no place but up from here. Glass half-full, baby! I meant every word of that statement, but what I didn't know was the weight it carried. Oh, how that negative script wrote itself all over my life. After a few awkwardly clumsy moments full of my jokey dodging tactics, I settled in and opened up.

My times with Lucy were both brutal and lifegiving all at once. She let me walk through rough moments when negative thoughts continued to play a loop in my mind, leaving me stuck. Like fog lifting on an early fall morning, it took a few sessions for clarity to come. I discovered the root issue, which was my own negative script playing in my mind.

Something is wrong with me.

Tears fell down my cheeks and onto my jeans as I admitted my discovery to Lucy. Words that I could barely get out of my mouth felt at home in my heart, like an unwanted and unnamed houseguest taking up residence even after the party is over. It was true—I've always felt this way. But why?

I've never been good at fitting in, sometimes not for lack of trying, but it seems instead I'm good at being different. Growing up, my grandpa would tease me every time we'd visit him. Like clockwork, at our first meal together (my grandma's ham balls, if we were lucky [heaven on a plate]), he'd see my hand grab the fork and pipe up, "Brittany, I'm right-handed, what are you?" After all the years, I knew our routine.

I'd reply, "I'm left-handed, Grandpa!"

Then he'd snicker, saying, "Brittany, if you're not right-handed, then what are you?" Confused, I'd look over to my parents, wishing they'd save me from this exchange.

"Grandpa, I'm left-handed." This would go on a few more times until I was certain the world had created a new label for this phenomenon of writing with one's left hand. In a gasp of defeat, I'd give up.

"If you're not right-handed, then you're *wrong*-handed!" And he'd laugh, proud of his dad joke. I, however, being the only lefty in my family, felt like something was wrong with me. Did he know this script was written over my heart? Not even in the slightest, but it's funny how moments like that happen without your permission, without your knowledge. Suddenly, you can't see past them.

In school, teachers would call me out for talking loudly in class: "Your voice just carries, Brittany." Boys always put me in the friend zone: "I'm sorry, Brittany; you're like one of the guys to me." Most days, I walked the halls of our campus in a T-shirt, basketball shorts, and flip-flops. Some days, I'd even show up in the scrubs I used years prior as a junior volunteer at our local hospital. Hot stuff, I know. I even boycotted makeup for a bit in high school because I told people I wanted a guy who would be happily surprised when I did wear it, not petrified when I didn't. They needed to know what they were getting themselves into. Feeling too much, too young, too old, too loud, too bossy, and so on felt like home to me. You name it, I was never "just right." And just like the children's story with Goldilocks and the three bears, I found myself as a pink-haired "Goldilocks" looking for her "just right" baby bear, to no avail. This didn't stop after high school, but man, how I wish it did. Who knew people

still act like high schoolers even as grown adults?! News to me. As
rejection came, situations became rough, friendships blew up, and
so on. These negative scripts played like a broken record in my head.
*It's your fault they don't want to be your friend. You are too loud
for people. Why can't you act like so-and-so?* You're no stranger to
this feeling, are you? And when we hear these scripts long enough,
we believe they must be true, and we allow them to take root deep
down. Just like that teenagers' summer camp small-group confes-
sion, everything clicked for me in the office with my counselor.
Something was wrong with me. That discovery felt like a fatal blow.
I had been knocked to the ground and was gasping for air. I had
been weighed and measured and was ultimately found wanting. But
that's not how the story ends. Like Paul writes in Philippians, "I'm
sure about this: the one who started a good work in you will stay
with you to complete the job by the day of Christ Jesus" (Phil. 1:6
CEB). We can trust that God, who finds you worthy of the sacrifice
of his own son, will be with you and help you see it for yourself.

- Do you feel like you aren't enough? If so, explain what makes
  you feel that way. (Maybe you too find yourself fighting for the
  best grades, friendships, looks, etc.)

_____

_____

_____

_____

- Let's write down the negative scripts that come to mind when
  we think about worth and the answers we wrote above.

_____

_____

_____

_____

Notes

1 *Dumb and Dumber*, directed by Peter Farrelly (Burbank, CA: New Line Cinema, 1994).

2 *A Knight's Tale*, directed by Brian Helgeland (Culver City, CA: Sony Pictures Releasing, 2001).

You are allowed
to be a
masterpiece
and a work in
progress
simultaneously.

—

SOPHIA BUSH

four

NEW SCRIPT

I Am Worthy

Trips to the store were a favorite activity of mine as a kid—not because I loved shopping but because I knew that I possessed the skills to talk my parents into a trip down the toy aisle during our outing. It's a gift I hold dear, and if you pay me enough, I may be able to teach you my ways. One day, during an outing to the store, I again sweet-talked my way down to the toy section. As we turned the corner from the beauty supply section, passing the bike racks, building blocks, and bouncy balls, we entered the aisle of stuffed animals. Heaven on earth, I tell you! So much fluff, color, and sweetness packed into one tiny section. My eyes skimmed over the lions and tigers and a bear . . . oh my. There she was—*my* bear. The bear had white silky fur and wore a plum velour pantsuit complete with a matching beret. Perfection in a bear, that's what she was. Grinning from ear to ear, I quickly grabbed her off the shelf as I bestowed the only name fitting a classy girl such as her: Samantha. I drank in her every detail and traced them out with my tiny fingers, and I promised Samantha that she and I would be inseparable. Until my mother informed me it was time to go and I needed to put back my bear. *My bear? Do you mean the stuffed animal of my dreams, my new best friend, my girl Samantha?!*

In all our trips to the store, I neglected to remember that our walks down the toy section involved more moments of looking and not necessarily buying. This was the flaw in my plan. I could convince the woman, my mom, to get there, but I never honed the craft of closing the sale. I always walked away empty-handed. How could I not bring Samantha home with me? Did my mother not see the instant bond we shared? She crushed my dreams of happiness. I did the only thing my little second-grade brain knew to do: squeeze Samantha tight and hide her. I dug deep into the shelf and buried her behind the other less-appealing animals—the laughable giraffe with the crazy long neck, the lion wearing glasses, and the puppy in a polka-dot dress. Surely, nobody would dig through all these to find my girl. My Samantha would stay there safely until she could come home with me.

As the holiday season approached, I never forgot about my lost friend trapped in the supermarket. Did she miss me? Was she OK? The days passed, and the Christmas tree in our living room began to be surrounded with beautifully wrapped presents. I inspected each gift and questioned its size, weight, and potential to house my best friend. Surely, she'd be under there in one of the packages. When Christmas morning came around, I ran into the living room, tore through my stocking from Santa, and watched my parents pass out everyone's gifts. The stack right in front of me held my Christmas fate. I anxiously bounced up and down in place, locking eyes on the one box that might have Samantha in it, clenching my fists and teeth as my body tensed with anticipation. Finally, my turn arrived, and I could open my gifts. I couldn't take it any longer. I snatched the box and ripped it to shreds. Paper flew, cardboard split, and there were uncontrollable squeals of a girl who had just opened the present of her dreams. Samantha! I embraced her in tears. She made it home. Her beauty far surpassed anything I remembered at the store. She was everything I ever wanted in one stuffed animal. Now almost thirty years later, this story sits fresh in my mind. Never had I wanted a gift so much in my life, and her anticipated arrival on Christmas morning filled me with joy.

Gifts are my love language. I love to give them, and I especially love receiving them. Truthfully, who doesn't love a good gift? For me, the best part of the actual gift is the moment before the receiver begins to open the package. The anticipation makes me want to bubble over with excitement, especially when I know I've picked out the perfect gift. But my excitement doesn't even compare with God's excitement on the day of your birth. Let me explain.

Think of it like this: at the beginning of time, God planned out the world. That included you, your life, and your future. Every single moment and detail was accounted for. He smiled at the thought of your laugh, his heart melted at how you would change the world, and he loved every bit of who he created you to be. Then after he planned the world, he sat back, grabbed a bowl of popcorn, and watched it unfold, waiting for the pinnacle moment of your arrival into the world. I can't be certain God sat and ate popcorn, but shoot, he's God! He can do whatever he wants. I like to think of him like this—eager and ready to see the gift of you. He is the same God who created the mountains, flung the stars into the galaxy, split the Grand Canyon, and hand-picked all the colors in South America's lush rainforests, and he thought, *Hmm, this world isn't complete without . . . you.*

Then when the day arrived for you to make your appearance in this world, he couldn't contain himself. He paced around in the delivery room, watched things happen, and checked on updates, eager to meet his girl. In true cinematic fashion, the moment you were born, time slowed down, almost to a standstill. People were whirling around and machines were beeping, but none of that mattered. Because here's what I know: your first breath took God's breath away. There you were, a miracle—his daughter, his beautiful baby girl. He had waited so long to see you, and now you were here. Tears filled his eyes as he looked upon your precious face. His love for you is instant and permanent. His love is not based on your accomplishments, if you stumble, or anything of the sort. You are the reason why he sent his son to die on the cross. He sent his son not out of guilt or shame but because his love compelled him. He didn't want to imagine life apart from you, his daughter, his beautiful baby girl. He had waited so long to see you. You are his special one, his favorite, a gift like no other. Wow.

My youngest crawled onto the bed and into my lap. With her head to my heart and her body tucked into mine, we sat in silence. Thoughts flooded my mind, but I had no clue how to put them into words and speak. While her father and I were out on a date a few hours earlier, she stayed home with her older siblings. This is something we did often because, thankfully, our kids are older and they can be trusted to hold down the fort for a short period. Or so we thought. That time, while we were out enjoying our dinner, she had become the object of mocking and pestering, so much so that she found herself hidden under the dining table, chairs pulled in tight, like her fort of safety. There she sat, broken and pleading for us to come home to rescue her.

Before we jump in further, I need you to know that I have great kids. Really and truly, they are the best. But as with all children, they are still working out the kinks of understanding when to stop, especially with the teasing. What they didn't know or take into account was Pippa's emotional barometer from the day. Tiredness from a previous late night, struggles with clothing (that's enough to put anyone in a bad mood, right?), and general insecurities boiled to the surface. When the siblings began to tease without end, she exploded and took comfort by hiding under a table.

There we were, curled up together, she and I with her daddy by her side. I took a deep breath, composed my thoughts, and tackled her broken spirit one word at a time. "Pippa, what do you think about your body?" That was a question I dreaded to hear answered because an eight-year-old shouldn't hate her body. Body image shouldn't be a struggle for anyone at any age, but especially not for an eight-year-old little girl. "I like it." The hesitation in her voice spoke louder than her words.

I replied, "Well, I think your body is pretty amazing, did you know that? You are super strong and make up the best dance moves. Your squishy cheeks and button nose bring a smile to my face. Your eyes of different colors show how unique you are. Your thick hair is stunning, especially with those gray patches. You are remarkable. But Pippa, my favorite part about you is your heart. You have a way of making people laugh, feel loved, and feel like they belong. That is something special." While her daddy and I thought the world of her, we wanted her to understand something important. We don't decide her worth or value. We don't have a say in whether she possesses beauty or talents. Only one gets to make that call, and that's God. Thankfully, her daddy and I agree with everything God has to say.

Grabbing my phone off the bed, I looked up a verse to share. My fingers naturally typed out the reference and immediately scrolled to it. This verse found its place on my lips often as I quoted it for my own heart. But while I could rattle it off without hesitation, I wanted her to read it for herself: "For we are God's masterpiece. He created us anew in Christ Jesus, so we can do the good things he planned for us long ago" (Eph. 2:10 NLT). It's right there in plain text: *we are God's masterpiece*. A masterpiece is a priceless work of art. She is a priceless work of art. As we continued to talk, I stroked her hair and told her that if people teased her or if she heard lies from the enemy, she needed to answer back. The only way to stop the negative dialogue is to find the truth and flip the script. In this case, the lie questioned her worth and value. I told her, "Anytime you hear statements that make you question your worth, whether from people or just in your mind, say this: 'That's a lie. I am God's masterpiece.'" Her precious cheeks curled up as a smile formed for the first time in hours. I couldn't stop the battle of her mind or even the words others might say about her, but I could point her to the one who could and then equip her with tools to fight.

Are you struggling too? For countless teens I've talked with, the answer is a booming yes. Like Pippa, I wish we could sit together, face-to-face, and I could tell you what God thinks of you. More importantly, I'd show you in his Word. You are God's masterpiece. Any statement that leads you to believe otherwise is a lie. Sometimes, when the enemy tries to speak lies over your life, it's easy to get flustered and feel like you need fancy words or actions to fight. It doesn't have to be complicated; it can be as simple as this script: *That's a lie. I am God's masterpiece.* Say it now, say it when you doubt, say it until you believe it. This is truth, and it is truth backed up by God's Word.

Stop and say it with me: *That's a lie. I am God's masterpiece.*

The idea of a masterpiece is interesting to me. Let me geek out for a second, OK? Looking through art history, one painting struck a chord with me. This piece didn't rest on a canvas—it filled the ceiling of the Sistine Chapel in the Vatican. Each year, around six million people tour the chapel and gaze upon this masterpiece. The artist responsible, Michelangelo, took four years to complete the painting. He spent more than thirty-five thousand hours working to bring his vision to life, so much so that his eyesight became permanently damaged. Can you imagine? Such work, detail, and precision went into that ceiling. Michelangelo gave his all, and hundreds of years later, we can still enjoy it.

Why is it easy for us to look at these pieces of work, made by man, and agree they are breathtaking, but when it comes to who we are, how we look, and how we estimate our worth, we feel more like a bargain store, mass-produced, tacky print? Forget the idea of a masterpiece; most of us don't feel worthy enough for the dollar bin at Target. The same pieces of art that many pay to see were created by brilliant artists who themselves were crafted by the ultimate artist: God. He is the reason any of this beauty exists. The thousands of hours Michelangelo spent on the Sistine Chapel can't even come close to the thought, effort, and time God put into creating you. Every detail was crafted with intention and love.

I think David sings it best in Psalm 139:

> You formed my innermost being, shaping my delicate
> inside and my intricate outside,
> and wove them all together in my mother's womb.
> I thank you, God, for making me so mysteriously complex!
> Everything you do is marvelously breathtaking.
> It simply amazes me to think about it!
> How thoroughly you know me, Lord!
> You even formed every bone in my body
> when you created me in the secret place;
> carefully, skillfully you shaped me from nothing to something.
> You saw who you created me to be before I became me!
> Before I'd ever seen the light of day,
> the number of days you planned for me
> were already recorded in your book.
> Every single moment you are thinking of me!
> How precious and wonderful to consider
> that you cherish me constantly in your every thought!
> O God, your desires toward me are more
> than the grains of sand on every shore!
> When I awake each morning, you're still with me.
>
> Psalm 139:13–18 TPT

David understood the love of God. He understood that God created us in complexity, that he has a plan for our life, and that we are always on his mind. Feeling known and loved in such a personal way helped David understand his worth and praise the One who made him so. God didn't limit his handiwork to David; these verses communicate how God sees me and how he sees you.

There is nothing accidental about your looks or your life. You are not a bargain-bin gal. You were created by the one who came up with the idea of a masterpiece. Would someone who didn't think you were worthy spend all this effort on you? Create you? Plan your life? Give you gifts and talents? Constantly think of you? No. You are worthy.

I know there's a tension between Jesus's sacrifice and us feeling worthy. No, we're not perfect yet. Yes, we needed Jesus to come and save us. But he did so because he deemed us worthy. In Scripture, we see that even before the foundation of the world, God planned this: "Even before he made the world, God loved us and chose us in Christ to be holy and without fault in his eyes" (Eph. 1:4 NLT). So let's settle that once and for all. He called you worthy. You are worthy. We've taken this idea of being "not worthy" too far. Nothing makes you unworthy. Your existence and that fact that you are treasured by God makes you worthy, no matter what.

- Old script: *I will never be enough.* New script: *God called me worthy enough to send his son to die for me* (John 3:16).

- Old script: *There is nothing special about me.* New script: *The God who created this world loves me immensely and calls me a daughter of a King* (2 Cor. 6:18).

- Old script: *My life doesn't matter.* New script: *God says that I am his masterpiece and that he had a plan for my life before I came to be* (Eph. 2:10).

- Old script: *I am worthless.* New script: *God says that I am his beloved child. I am worthy of his inheritance and treasures because I am his true child* (Rom. 8:16–17).

☾ It's Time for Your Glow Up!

What are some scripts you need to flip? Below, write them out and ask God to help you flip them. You can also look through your Bible, maybe google verses dealing with this topic, or even ask trusted friends, family, or leaders to help you.

Old Script: _____

New Script: _____

Old Script: _____

New Script: _____

Old Script: _____

New Script: _____

☾ Grab a Mirror

See the girl staring back at you. Take a second to take her in, all of her. Thank her, tell her you're proud of how far she's come, tell her that you believe in her, tell her that she's worth it, and bestie, tell her that you love her. It may seem fake at first, something you do in the moment, but over time, you'll believe it.

☾ Ask God

Take a second and ask God a question: *What is your favorite thing about me?* Then just listen. Do you know that God is excited about you? You aren't a disappointment to him; you aren't someone he just deals with. No, you are his prized treasure. I've noticed that often the thing I'm most insecure about or try to downplay most is the thing that he brings to my mind. It's almost like a reminder:

Hey, I created you just like this! I love it so much, don't hide! Stop right now, quiet your mind and heart, and ask God: *What is your favorite thing about me?*

Write down what he shows you.

Take Them at Their Word

How do you receive compliments? If you are anything like me, you are an expert dodger and can discredit most kind words spoken in your direction. When it comes to family and close friends, I claim they have an obligation to speak that way. When an acquaintance or someone from a distance praises me, I deflect, assuming they don't know me well enough to say those things. There is never a win or compliment I believe. You too? Try something new, and don't dart, dodge, or disprove their statements. Take them at their word. Yes, it's easy to see the flaws in yourself and believe that your flaws are the truth. Why can you trust compliments? Family and friends know you so well and can call out all the beauty in you. They've traveled the miles with you, done the hard work, and stuck with you. Praise the Lord! Who better to know and speak the truth over you?! Acquaintances and people see your positives in passing, online, and at a distance and just want to speak life over you. Whether you agree or not, you've made an impression on them. Let them show you how the world sees you.

- Ask a close friend or family member what's something good they see in you. Then write their answer below. Remember this compliment!

_____

- Do you remember something positive a stranger or acquaintance has said about you? Write it below and choose to believe it! Remember, they didn't have to stop and say these things. They chose to!

_____

♔ Finish the Statement

Conclude your negative script with the words *but God made me worthy*. If the statement you're believing leaves you feeling worthless, then it isn't the truth. Again, try following the troubling scripts with this refrain: *but God made me worthy*.

Try this out: write two phrases and then finish the statement.

_____, but God made me worthy.

_____, but God made me worthy.

This is my prayer for you as this chapter closes. It is a declaration that I hope sticks in your mind, floods your heart, and allows truth to sink in.

glow up
DECLARATION

Your worth is not negotiable.
No job, no circumstance, no title,
and no man can decide it.
You are worthy just as you are
and just because you are.
You've been designed with master
precision by a creator who is
mad about you.
So much so that your first breath
took his breath away.
You are the definition of worth
and value, and you are
more than enough.
Now lift your head high.

five

I Fail in Comparison to Others

"What a friend we have in Jesus."

That was the thought rolling around in my head as my heart skipped a beat, and my face turned the perfect shade of crimson. This golden bronzed, chiseled, sixteen-year-old guy walked my way with his gorgeous brown shaggy hair that flowed like Zac Efron's in *High School Musical*. He completely distracted me from my theater assignment, which was probably one of the few classes I paid attention to and took seriously in school.

Get'cha head in the game, Brittany. Snap out of it; pay attention.

Let me tell you about this boy, because I don't think you understand. Have you ever had a crush on someone? Surely, I'm not the only one cursed with the teenage hormones that led me to see greasy, stinky, teenage boys with giant heart-filled eyes. But this boy, he was something special. I loved everything about him. His warm, caring eyes, his constantly smiling face with the cutest dimples, and his perfectly playful laugh got me every time. Sam proved to be a rare breed in our high school. He not only sported the title of high school jock on the football and track teams but also loved to sing, earning himself a spot in the highest-ranking choir at our school and many times in our state. The only problem? Every girl in the school seemed to have a crush on him as well. Great, how was this very average, crazy theater girl supposed to catch the attention of this Greek god in human form? I didn't stand a chance. That I was sure of.

All the other girls were smart, beautiful, charming, or could sing beautifully. They would follow him to class flirting endlessly, crowd around him in the choir hall just to eat lunch near him, and command his attention. They seemed to possess the upper hand, and competing against them felt like the classic David-versus-Goliath fight. The one thing I had going for me? I was a scrappy girl and wouldn't admit defeat. So I hatched a plan.

One day when I overheard Sam talking with one of his friends about something track related, I interjected myself into the conversation. To my surprise, they kept talking with me, and before long I began to brag about my own track skills. I threw out stats and times of my own accomplishments, which I honestly had no clue what any of it meant. But I didn't stop; I couldn't. Sam looked intrigued. "I bet I could beat you." I blurted out without even thinking about the words before I said them. "Oh really? Then meet me after school and let's see about that." And with a simple "you're on," I found myself locked into a race with my crush.

This might be a good time to share this piece of information—I wasn't on the track team. And I never ran. In my blind, heart-eyes, hormonal haze, I challenged a "professional athlete" to a race I was destined to lose. Shoot.

When I showed up to the field after Sam finished track practice, a crowd appeared ready to cheer on their man. Apparently, the talk of practice that afternoon was about a girl named Brittany who could outrun anyone. *What did I get myself into?* So I quickly hatched another plan. Right after one of our peers signaled *go*, I took off as fast as I could and "tripped." Sam ran to the finish line and puffed up his chest, screaming as he celebrated his win. There I sat, defeated and humiliated on the track, ready to hide in a hole forever. Now he definitely wouldn't pick me. (Except he did.)

As funny and embarrassing as that story is, I know that many of you have felt the same way. Always looking and measuring yourself against the person next to you, comparing lives, clothes, grades, friends, and so on just struggling to find a place to belong. *If I could just be like her, then the guy would pay attention to me. If I had these clothes, then I'd make more friends. If I could just play it cool, I wouldn't always look like a fool. If I was just smart, then I wouldn't struggle on my tests.* You'll never win trying to weigh your life against someone else's. This I am sure of.

It's amazing how easily negative words come to mind while remembering truth seems impossible. In our house, we call the negative statements sticky words, because they hold on for dear life. Once at work, I watched Sam and his friend toss mini squishy animals toward the ceiling. The goal was to be the first to make yours stick. It took a few attempts, but both guys successfully stuck their animals. However, now that they were on the ceiling, we had no way of getting them down. The guys chucked items up to the ceiling tiles hoping to knock down the tiny animals, all to no avail. Those suckers would not budge. For months, we randomly tried to get them down until, finally, one fell. Though it no longer clung to the ceiling, it left an unsightly oily residue in its place, like a marker saying, *I will not be forgotten.* Negative scripts are like those sticky animals. They are thrown up in haste, and they are extremely hard to get rid of.

Do you know what age researchers say that people start dealing with comparison? At age five. Five years old. And if I'm being honest, what I'm learning is that adults all the way into their seventies are still dealing with the idea of comparison. What this should tell you is that you're not alone. Every single person walking this earth is or has or will struggle with comparing themselves to those around them. It just feels so much bigger, harder, and more threatening as a teenager.

Molly and I met often to talk about this exact thing. Getting to hang out with teens like her are some of my favorite times because I basically get to be the cool aunt. As a teenager it's hard to want to always open up to your parents when they are too close to the "problem" and their listening can be clouded with "answers." But with me, I'm just the cool, pink-haired, tattooed adult friend who can be a sounding board to help you walk through the areas where you feel stuck. That's when teens meet with me most—when they feel stuck. Whether they are stuck in fear, sadness, anxiety, or even comparison. We have a neutral and nonjudgmental place to lay everything out on the table and see where to go from there. Most of the time we'd chat at a local Chick-fil-A over a sweet tea and ice cream cone or in the Sonic drive-thru.

The negative script of comparison filled Molly's mind day after day. As a high school student, she was starting to think about college and her future. Molly had dreams of getting into a college out of state, one far away from the safety of home but exciting all the same. We talked dreams, plans, and how she was the perfect fit for this school. Then we put together a plan to help her succeed. One that highlighted all the areas she excelled in and uniquely shined. Deep in my heart, I believed Molly had the ability to make a difference in this world. Others looked at her and saw a leader, a trailblazer, and someone full of confidence. This is not what Molly saw in herself. She constantly pointed out her weakness and compared her dreams and goals to others'. It devastated me that Molly couldn't see what she had to offer and stop measuring it up to those around her.

One day, a week before her college essay was due, we met and worked on her paper together. We had a fun angle on the generic topic given. All she had to do was go home and write it out. But when Molly got home, something different happened. After talking with her parents, she started to question everything. These things happen often with dreams and fun ideas in the early stage; we bring too many people into the equation, and when they don't share our same excitement and enthusiasm, we believe it's rejection. Ideas are just so vulnerable. And when we feel that way, we start looking around at everyone else doing all the things and compare our dreams and ideas to theirs. *Does this idea make sense? What if I'm not heading in the right direction? How can I do it any better than so-and-so? I might as well just give up.* Satan is tricky like that. He sits quietly while you dream and plan with the cheers and support of others around you, ready to lift you up and propel you forward. Then in the silence of your own space, or through the questions of others, he starts to whisper the lies. Soon, you forget all the breakthroughs and excitement and sit defeated, wishing that you could somehow measure up.

Each perfectly poised and styled photo square on Instagram reminded a client, Kara, of where she failed, what she didn't look like, and things she needed to complete herself. A fun site meant to connect people around the world now caused her to feel crushed, alone, and lacking. Kara and I loved to meet and chat over coffee. As she twirled the straw through the whipped cream on her iced coffee, Kara shared more of her struggle with social media and how it made her feel. How could this beautiful girl feel so broken and unappealing?

Social media isn't a bad place, and for the most part, I love it. But as a grown woman, it has, from time to time, led to me feeling awful about my body, talents, and life. Because of that, I can't even imagine how it's affecting young girls. One day, after a devastating conversation with Kara, I searched for answers. One study said that 63 percent of teens show a significant decrease in self-esteem after only one month on social media. After only one month. This explains how Kara had gotten to such a low point. But she's not the only one. According to the study, over half the population is. I'd bet my life savings (which is all of five dollars) that social media is hurting them all. People picture their lives and try to see if they measure up to what others are posting. Are they thin enough? Pretty enough? On trend according to the newest fashion? If not, how can they fix it?

For Kara, her comparison surfaced most in dealing with body image. *My face is hideous. I weigh too much. No guy will ever like me.* Confronted with all the thin, seemingly perfect women, she found herself stuck listening to scripts claiming she wasn't good enough. Then our conversation took an unexpected turn; she confessed to some serious eating disorders. She explained how eating food made her hate herself. Sometimes, she'd remember all the other girls she longed to measure up to, and before she knew it, Kara found herself in the bathroom puking. Each trip to the bathroom left her feeling more empty, full of shame, and further from her goal of happiness. Her face fell into her palm as she turned from me and toward the window. After a few seconds of silence, she whispered through her hand, "Why am I not good enough?" Tears filled my eyes as my jaw clenched trying to keep some sense of composure. Oh, how I wanted to climb over the table and hug her, never to let go. She lost herself in the lives of others, and in trying to be like them, she lost how amazing she was. I knew this feeling all too well. How could I help her see these things? How could we get her out of the comparison trap?

Social media isn't the root. This struggle, the one of comparison, is as old as time. We see it even in Genesis with the story of Rachel and Leah. Jacob, forced to leave his family because he deceived his brother and caused quite a mess, went to live and work with his uncle. As he neared the land of his uncle, he noticed a woman off in the distance. She was one of the most beautiful women he had ever seen. Her name was Rachel, and within a few minutes of being around her, "Jacob kissed Rachel, and he wept aloud" (Gen. 29:11 NLT). Can you imagine being so smitten with someone that you not only kiss her within a few minutes of meeting her but also are brought to tears from the emotion of it all?

A few months passed, and Jacob had worked his heart out helping his uncle, Laban. One night at dinner, Laban, feeling guilty about all the free labor, asked how he could repay Jacob. They struck a deal. Jacob would work for seven years to have Rachel's hand in marriage. Time flew by quickly for Jacob as he worked those years. "But his love for her was so strong that it seemed to him but a few days" (Gen. 29:20 NLT). Love is the ultimate motivator. For Jacob, the time didn't dissuade him. Rather, it caused his love to strengthen.

Finally, the day arrived for Jacob and Rachel to be married. I'm sure if it were to take place in modern times, this would be a TLC special where we gawk at floral arrangements, *ooh* over wedding sites, and *ah* over the wedding party's attire. Laban threw a big feast as a celebration, and once everyone was full, drunk, and happy, he snuck Leah into Jacob's tent to seal the marriage deal. *Wink, wink.* "Who's Leah?" you may be asking. Just Rachel's older sister and one about whom the Bible says, "There was no sparkle in Leah's eyes, but Rachel had a beautiful figure and a lovely face" (Gen. 29:17 NLT). Ouch. There seemed to be nothing fancy or attractive about Leah, but all the adoration was saved for Rachel. Can you imagine being the older sister, the one who is supposed to marry first, but nobody wants to marry you? Apparently, things looked desperately grim because Laban, Leah's father, felt as though he needed to deceive someone into marrying her. My heart breaks for Leah because I'm sure she always found herself vying for attention, craving affection, and constantly competing and comparing herself with her younger sister.

I have two younger sisters, and sometimes it's hard to not find myself in comparison with them. I've been where Leah was. My younger sister was the pretty one, not me. She was born on my first birthday and was a constant source of comparison and competition.

While we joke about it now, and while I love having a birthday buddy, there were seasons when it crushed me to feel like I needed to measure up to her. Or worse, when others chose her, the pretty one, over me, the ugly but funny one. Growing up in school, there were always the pretty girls, the smart girls, and the athletic girls. Sometimes you found a type of girl who was both pretty *and* something else. Those were the "Rachels." Dang those girls. Quickly, I decided to be the funny girl. Because if I was the funny girl, I'd be able to make fun of myself before anyone else ever could. That part came easy for me. I laughed my way through years of awkwardness, including high school and into adulthood, until all I was left with were fragile, broken pieces in a tough but hilarious exterior. I couldn't forget those negative scripts.

I wonder if Leah tried to play the funny girl on the morning after she married Jacob. He woke up to quite the shock, which quickly turned into anger. I'm sure that didn't comfort Leah. I wonder if she too tried to crack a joke in hopes of diffusing her pain, maybe with a quick "April fools!" or "Oops, you mean this isn't my tent?" I cringe as I think of how hard that morning had to have been for her, and then to hear her father and new husband argue over Rachel. *Why can't I be pretty like Rachel, wanted like Rachel?* After all the arguing, Laban agreed to let Jacob marry Rachel if he promised to work for another seven years. The only stipulation: wait until the bridal week passes because, you know, he *just* married the sister.

My heart breaks for those sisters. An undeniable wedge found itself between them, and it only grew into bitterness and resentment. They found themselves in constant comparison and fighting for the love and attention of anyone around them, especially Jacob. The negative scripts Leah believed ran deep. They were probably started by her father, echoed through her sister, and made even louder through the fact that Jacob never loved her. It's painfully clear when we see Leah strive so hard to bring love and honor to her family by providing Jacob with a son. Each name for her baby boy was cloaked in suffering because, after every name, she longed for love and acceptance. Reuben, "The LORD has noticed my misery, and now my husband will love me" (Gen. 29:32 NLT); Simeon, "The LORD heard that I was unloved and has given me another son" (Gen. 29:33 NLT); Levi, "Surely this time my husband will feel affection for me, since I have given him three sons!" (Gen. 29:34 NLT); and Zebulun, "God has given me a good reward. Now my husband will treat me with respect, for I have given him six sons" (Gen. 30:20 NLT). There was such pain and longing to feel loved. Do you see it? Maybe you resonate with how Leah felt when you compare yourself to others, try to live up to their expectations, and constantly chase their approval. These scripts leave you in such pain, feeling lonely and defeated. *Why can I never be good enough? What's wrong with me? Why can't I be like them?*

As I said, I know this pain too. But here's what I also know: someone did see Leah's plight and cared for her greatly. She didn't need to strive, compete, or even measure up for his affection. That someone was God, and while others left her to the side, forgetting she mattered, he had a special plan for her. She was a part of his great rescue plan to save the whole world. Through Leah came the lineage of Jesus. He picked her especially for the job. What an honor. Just like the Lord saw and cared for Leah, he sees and cares for you. His heart breaks as you listen to negative scripts pressuring you to measure up, compare with, or strive.

Comparison can leave you broken, striving, and wanting for more. Fearful life has passed you by; it makes you believe good things only happen to other people. This is a lie; don't let these pain-ful thoughts stick. There is truth to be found, and it often comes in a whisper. Let God pull you in close and share the truth Paul spoke of in Romans: "For the Holy Spirit makes God's fatherhood real to us as he whispers into our innermost being, 'You are God's beloved child!'" (Rom. 8:16 TPT). You are his beloved child, and there is no one you need to fight against or compare with for that honor. It's already yours.

- Have you ever found yourself stuck in comparison? What happened? How did it feel?
- We read about the story with Jacob, Rachel, and Leah. Have you ever felt like a Leah?
- Let's write down the negative scripts that come to mind when we think about comparison and the stories we read in this chapter.

_____

_____

_____

_____

_____

You are
God's
beloved
child!

—

ROMANS 8:16 TPT

six

NEW SCRIPT

I Am Not Held Hostage by Comparison

There is this rage and phenomenon among many teen girls your age. "What is it?" you may be asking. It's the one and only Taylor Swift. Yes, I see the smirk on your face. I have one too, even typing out her name. If you're not a fan of Taylor Swift—or a Swiftie, as we like to call ourselves—you're missing out. Listen, I'm not one to jump on a craze because everyone else is doing it, or as the saying goes, I won't jump off a cliff just because everyone else is. Being an individual is fun for me, and I like the shock and awe when people react to my not liking something culture is raving about. Case in point—Star Wars. I have never watched a movie, not one. Maybe this isn't a big deal for a kid your age, but for an adult, this is a big deal. People usually reply with a "Why not?" when I inform them of my lack of desire to ever watch one of the films. Maybe I'd like them, who knows at this point? But now I kind of like the whole exchange because I didn't jump on the trend.

This works for me, until it doesn't. Like when I miss out on all the wonder, joy, and fanfare that is Taylor Swift. Not long ago the internet blew up with people purchasing tickets for Taylor's Eras Tour as they almost instantly sold out. Fans were elated when they scored a coveted spot; others slammed their hands on the counter as they missed the moment in securing one, then proceeded to beg anyone and everyone to sell them theirs. This whole ordeal caused me to roll my eyes in disbelief because I didn't understand—that is, until months later, when these fans began to post videos of their concert experiences. The fun and excitement was fascinating to me and honestly gave me a severe case of FOMO. Have you ever heard of FOMO? It's an acronym that stands for "fear of missing out." And these videos from Taylor's tour gave me major FOMO. I wanted to be there and experience the room, her singing, her costumes, and her showmanship. But I missed it.

Not long after that, I had the chance to watch the Eras Tour in a local movie theater. This time I made sure to grab a ticket—and of course four more for my daughters—but deep down inside I was a little nervous that after all the buildup, I'd be disappointed. Either way, we were going, and my girls were excited. Each of us planned Taylor themed outfits full of sparkles, sequins, and of course, our best-friend bracelets, which had different song and album titles on them. The movie experience was as close to the actual live concert a person could ask for. Unlike going to watch a normal movie, attendees—Swifties—would stand up, dancing and singing along, filling all the open spaces of the room. It didn't take long before I found myself joining the crowd as I tried to keep up with the songs I knew and danced my heart out like I wasn't a middle-aged woman. At the end of the night, as I sat in the car driving my girls home while they couldn't stop talking about the experience, I began to think about this girl, Taylor Swift. She doesn't know me, and she probably never will (Wouldn't it be cool if we met one day?), but I learned a lot from her that night. Here's a summary of what I learned from Taylor, and you can too:

- Don't listen to the haters or naysayers. Taylor's journey has not been an easy one. She's run into her fair share of naysayers. But the beauty is that she's never let it stop her. Don't let the negative voices and crowd keep you from what you love. Pull a T-Swift and shake it off. Because guess what? The haters gonna hate, hate, hate, hate, hate.

- Do it your OWN special way. Too many times we try to fit the mold, follow what others have done, or go with the norm. But what if the key to our success is actually embracing our own unique qualities and running with them? Taylor is proof of this. She knows who she is, and she OWNS it! It's time for you to do the same.

- Work hard, but have fun! There is no doubt that Taylor has worked her tail off writing songs, creating albums, and performing her tours across the globe. Many months, days, and hours—blood, sweat, and tears—are put into the experiences she creates for us. The girl is busy! But when she takes the stage, you can see it in her face: she's having fun. It's OK to work hard, but don't take life too seriously, and have a little fun.

- Sparkle is *always* a good idea. No explanation needed, just add sparkle.

"If you're lucky enough to be different, never change."—Taylor Swift

I want you to see that you have your own unique life, skills, talents, and future. I'm saying it, and so is Taylor. The biggest waste of your time would be to spend your days trying to keep up with other people, do what they're doing, and compare yourself to them. Pull a T-Swift and chart your own path, your own unique way, with all you've got. To do anything less would be a loss.

A few years ago, we discovered that one of our daughters, Paisley, has dyslexia. While testing her, the school found her comprehension to be off the charts, but she struggled to read the words. If you asked Paisley, the words appeared to be jumbled and moving around, and

some letters even shapeshifted into others. It's a challenge for her to figure out and decode the real word at times.

The night we found out about her diagnosis, Sam and I sat her down to share it with her. We were armed with encouraging words, facts, and even famous people she loved who also had the same diagnosis, including Albert Einstein, Jim Carrey, and Walt Disney. Our goal as her parents was to create a positive dialogue around the subject. We didn't want our daughter to feel inferior, different, or ashamed about any of this. But we knew that meant we had to show her how special she truly was.

As we discussed this with Paisley, her facial expression shifted from bright and bubbly to guarded and fearful. "Mom, sometimes I feel different and even bad, like I'm not smart enough, strong enough, brave enough. I'm just different from my friends at school," she said. She went on to explain how sometimes she would go into her class at school with a fun hairstyle but that some kids would laugh at her so she'd quickly pull it down and "fix" it. Then as tears filled her eyes, she added, "Now I'm going to stand out because I can't read. I'm not brave like you, Mom. I can't be like you." Her words shattered my heart. Tears poured down my cheeks and onto my shirt. Then after a brief moment, I choked back the tears and pulled her in close to my chest.

"Paisley, part of that is true," I said. "Part of that is your mom being brave. I do look different from other people. I have tattoos, piercings, pink hair, and lots of kids. In a lot of ways, I stand out, and the cards are stacked against me. But there's another part of me that feels like a mess. I'll look to your dad and question things that I've said or done. Was it OK? Was it weird?

"But here's the thing: I will never look like everyone else, and the brave part of me is OK with that. When I struggle to feel brave, I check in with people I know and love to keep encouraging me to show up bravely. But God helps me the most to be brave. I just have to be OK with being different. You, honey, were never meant to blend in with everyone else, and you have to be brave enough to realize that. And in the moments you struggle, you come to people like your dad and me to remind you of that."

I wanted so desperately for this precious girl to know and see what we all saw. She didn't need to be like everyone else, and she didn't need to fit or measure up to anyone's standards. She just needed to be Paisley. This girl could change the world, but first she'd need to stop trying to compare herself with others. That night, as we wrapped up our talk with her, her demeanor shifted. What began as fear and anxiety ended with pride and bravery. Paisley understood who she was and where to go when she struggled to remember.

A few days later, Paisley and I were on a walk, just the two of us. It's always fun to get one-on-one time with each kid, and walks with this girl often leave me lacking words. Out of the blue, she turned to me and said, "Mom, do you want to know what my favorite word is? My favorite word is *yet*."

My face perplexed, I asked, "Why is that, honey?"

Her answer stopped me right in my tracks: "Because my teacher has a sign up in our classroom that says, 'Believe in the power of yet,' and I love it so much. When things are hard, you have to remember you may not be the best *yet*, or that this isn't easy *yet*, or that you're not strong *yet*. But Mom, there's always a yet. You just have to keep trying." Dang. Y'all, she was nine years old, but clearly she was light-years ahead of me on this whole personal growth deal. Every day is a new lesson with this girl, and I've often said I want to be Paisley when I grow up. She loves all people, believes in the good of everyone, and has fierce confidence that God can do anything. Her ability to push through hard things (like dyslexia) and persevere is inspiring. She is unapologetically charting her path and doing it her way. I love every bit of it.

Which brings me to you. Follow the path marked out for you. Not against anyone but at your pace, for your people, fueled by your passions. The writer in Hebrews states,

Therefore, since we are surrounded by such a huge crowd of witnesses to the life of faith, let us strip off every weight that slows us down, especially the sin that so easily trips us up. And let us run with endurance the race God has set before us. We do this by keeping our eyes on Jesus, the champion who initiates and perfects our faith. (Heb. 12:1–2 NLT)

Life is just like a race, marked and planned out for each one of us. Just like with Taylor and her millions of cheering fans, we are also surrounded by and reminded of those who came before us: people written about in the Bible, who through flaws, failures, and lackluster lives held onto faith and changed the world. They ran their own races, and through their examples, coupled with the Word of God, we can too. Like Paisley, we need people right beside us, in real time, ready to cheer us on and lift us up. They can help us flip the negative comparison script and see our failures and challenges differently. When we reframe that narrative, those struggles look more like *yets*. There's always a yet; you just have to keep trying. (Thank you, Paisley.)

One morning, as our family sat in the dining room eating breakfast, Sam came over and kissed my forehead. That's our standard parting practice. It's cute, I know. Then Sam turned to the kids, waved bye, and headed out the door for work. Before he made it out of the house, Pippa yelled out to him, "God is awesome, and so are you!" Sam smirked, waved again, and shut the door behind him. This sentence is a staple in the Estes household. Usually, it's one spoken over our kids by Sam or myself as they head out to school, along with a quick addendum to the statement: "and make wise choices." However, that day, our littlest one spoke it over us.

Years ago, Sam and I realized something significant. We influence how our kids start their days. School is tough, friendships are hard, and navigating all the dynamics of growing up can be a challenge. But the last thing they hear and how we set them up to tackle the day as they walk away is *God is awesome*. We hope that they will remember who he is, what he is capable of, and that he's on their side so that no matter what they face, that truth remains. He is a big God, and he is with them. The second part of the phrase is *you're awesome too*. The same God who created the whole world created you. He doesn't make mediocre, unimportant things. No, he creates wonderful masterpieces who are full of special skills, talents, and passions. In light of this truth, we want our children to live big, bold, and bright lives for God, because he thinks they are awesome too.

Guess what? It's sinking in for them. The words we speak over our children matter. Friends, the scripts we speak over ourselves matter too. So bestie, I want to say the same to you today, wherever you are: **God is awesome, and so are you.** Read that again. Maybe you should even write it down on a card and tape it on your mirror as a daily reminder.

And here's the crazy thing. The girl next to you who you always compare yourself to is awesome too. Let her shine. Let her do her thing so you can do yours. You aren't falling behind or needing to run past her. She is an incredible wonder, just like you. But the longer you find yourself chasing after what she's doing, the further you may be getting from the life, direction, and pace God has in store for you. Let him be awesome in you!

A couple of weeks ago, I had a group of girls over at my house. The morning before they came over, I realized that some of these gals whom I had never met might be fretting over what to wear. The reason I knew this was because I would be too if I were in their place. Days prior, when I invited them, I told them the attire was comfy. But you know as well as I do that means *very* different things for different people. Am I right?! It's silly, but as women, this is something we think about, and I was not about to let these ladies spend the morning in a tizzy trying to strategically pick out the perfect outfit, one they spent forever trying on, accessorizing, and staring at in the mirror but had to appear to be thrown together. You know, the *I-woke-up-like-this* look—except you didn't. With that in mind, I sent a picture of myself in leggings and a giant sweatshirt with the following text out to the ladies: "Because we're girls and this is a thing, when I say comfy, I really mean comfy. No need to dress to impress, unless that's how you roll!" I wanted them to know there is never a standard to be around me. Let me squash that comparison game before it starts. Because truthfully, I'm not interested in surface-level constant competition and keeping up appearances. I want messy, authentic people because I'm one of them. What if people felt they had the freedom to show up as themselves—bedhead, sweatshirts, and all? On the good days, bad days, and every day in between? What if they could be real about the messy parts? What if you could do the same? You might just help someone feel seen and give them the freedom to stop competing or comparing.

I have a cool theory. You will shine brighter when you cheer on the girl next to you. It's true. Anytime I'm coaching teens and we touch on the comparison struggle, I offer this solution to help them flip the script in their minds. The comparison game doesn't have to be the wedge we create between us and them. You will shine brighter when you cheer on the girl next to you. It's a wedge we create between us and others. Besties, the enemy is lying to us and making us believe in scarcity, not abundance. If we operate in scarcity, then we see those around us as competition fighting on opposing teams instead of companions fighting together. Scarcity says there isn't enough, but abundance says there is way more than enough. The comparison game is a trap and a deadly one at that. It sends you into a frenzy of negative thoughts, letting you believe you don't measure up and don't have your act together. Ultimately, you find yourself trapped and lost in bitterness. Let's just call comparison what it truly is: sin. Yikes. But it's true. In the New Testament, James writes of the effects of sin:

> Temptation comes from our own desires, which entice us and drag us away. These desires give birth to sinful actions. And when sin is allowed to grow, it gives birth to death. So don't be misled, my dear brothers and sisters. Whatever is good and perfect is a gift coming down to us from God our Father, who created all the lights in the heavens. (James 1:14–17 NLT)

Comparison gives birth to death, and no good can come from it. So instead of allowing my clients to stay trapped in comparison, we take a new route. We call out the things we see in others, and we thank God that he is a good Father and an excellent gift giver. Because we know he's a loving Father and good gift giver, that means he won't leave us empty-handed. A shift happens in their minds when they begin to see others through this lens, when they let go of scarcity and allow abundance to pour in. Here's how abundance happens through cheering:

- You take your eyes off yourself and begin supporting a girl doing her thing, running her race, and making a change.

- You show others around you how it's done; they don't have to compare either. You lead the way and remind them that we can *all* win.

- You aren't wasting your time and energy plotting and scheming to try to beat the next girl. You'd be surprised at how much creativity is killed when you chase someone else's life. Creativity is priceless; use it on yourself.

- You aren't full of stress and desperation to figure out what works for her because you've adopted a new motto: *You do you, boo.*

- You realize that you have your special flair to bring to the table, something no one else has. Don't lose sight of this.

Listen, we are better together. I will say this until there isn't any more breath in my lungs. But we can't work together if we continue to compare. Stop looking at "her" and feeling inadequate. You are the girl God chose for such a time as this, to do the work he has just for you—not for some other woman because she has her own mission! Don't fall for the scripts causing you to compare your life to others.

The struggle in looking around at others and trying to measure up is this: we weren't created to make people our standard. Paul understood this well and even challenged the church in Corinth with this idea: "Oh, don't worry; we wouldn't dare say that we are as wonderful as these other men who tell you how important they are! But they are only comparing themselves with each other, using themselves as the standard of measurement. How ignorant!" (2 Cor. 10:12 NLT). Paul understood the assignment; he didn't live for the approval of others. We can do the same; let's make God our standard. It's not that we are aiming for perfection, but we strive to mimic his example and live out his teaching. He's OK with that—are you? Let's take a hard look at the scripts we speak over ourselves when we compare ourselves to other classmates, neighbors, celebrities, and so on. What does Jesus want to do with the script that we don't measure up to? With what truth can we counter the script that says we're behind or not exactly where we're meant to be? Let's speak truth over these negative scripts:

- Old script: *I will never measure up.* New script: *The Holy Spirit inside of me reminds me that I am God's beloved child* (Rom. 8:16).

- Old script: *There is no place for me.* New script: *God says that I am an integral part of the body of Christ, and not only do I have a place, but I am needed* (1 Cor. 12:12–27).

- Old script: *It will never be my turn.* New script: *Through God's strength, I can continue doing good and will see the reward if I do not give up* (Gal. 6:9).

- Old script: *I can't compete against her.* New script: *God has given me all the qualifications I need to run my own race* (2 Cor. 3:4–5).

⚜ It's Time for Your Glow Up!

What are some scripts you need to flip? Below, write them out and ask God to help you flip them. You can also look through your Bible, maybe google verses dealing with this topic, or even ask trusted friends, family, or leaders to help you.

Old Script: _____

New Script: _____

Old Script: _____

New Script: _____

Old Script: _____

New Script: _____

⚜ Play

Your soul was created to play. Did you know that? As we grow older, we learn to take everything seriously, and we turn our talents, skills, and passions into monetary gain. That isn't inherently wrong, but along the way, we forget what it means to just play, to simply create just to create, to play just for the fun of it. We need to find our sense of play again. Try one thing today that brings you back to a state of play. Take the pressure off yourself. This will help flip the script in your mind that everything needs a success rate, comparison marker, or deadline. Nope, not today. It's all about the play.

- What's something you love to do? I don't mean sitting on the couch watching TV; no, I want you to think of an activity that brings you life. Do you like to draw, play a sport, sing? What is it? Write down your answer, and write why you like it. Then make space this week to play!

Cheer a Sister On

Give a sister a little shout-out. This can start a chain reaction not only in your heart but in the hearts of women all around. If they see you being vocal about your support and love for the girl next to you, they will join in too. Let's reassure them that it's OK to love and cheer each other on. This is huge, and it starts with you. Can you be the change?

- Who are five girls in your circle of influence who you can cheer on? Think about ways to encourage them.

Limit Your Intake

Take some time away from social media. Look, I get it—I am a huge fan of all things social media. But I also know that it can lead to an anxious and discontent heart for me. I'm guessing this might be true for you as well. It's extremely easy to see what others are doing, wearing, and creating and then try to hold our lives up to that standard. Comparing our lives to others' leaves us feeling lost and less than. Instead of settling for the highs and lows brought on by the social media comparison game, let's be proactive. Take a break and shut it all down. Focus on the people around you. Fun fact: it's hard to know what you're supposedly missing or what you should supposedly be measuring up to when you can't see it.

Lead with Gratitude

My encouragement to you is to start a gratitude journal. My friend shared once about how she keeps a journal by her bed. Each night, she grabs it and writes at least three things she is grateful for. Sometimes the list reads of big wins from the day, while others are simple things. At first, she said coming up with a list challenged her, but as the days passed, it was easier to see things stick out. That's because she flipped the script. Subconsciously, she told her mind, *We're going to look for the good*, and over time, it became more natural. Throw out the comparison and fill it with gratitude.

- Let's start right now. What are three things you're grateful for in this moment?

Working to break the scripts of comparison may feel daunting and tough. I don't want you to miss your life because you're too busy trying to chase down someone else's. And I definitely don't want you to feel stuck because you struggle to see how you can win in your life. You are never stuck; don't agree with that lie. Don't let those damaging scripts take hold inside your heart.

glow up
DECLARATION

Sister, you don't need to compare.
You are not behind,
less than, or needing to strive
for your place.
You have your own special gifts,
for this season, at this moment.
So cheer the girl next to you on.
She needs your support,
just like you need hers.
Remember, God is awesome,
and so are you.
Now shine as you were made to.

seven

OLD SCRIPT

I Am Broken by Loneliness

When I entered kindergarten, I believed that I was hot stuff. I was one of the cool kids now that I could go to school. Oh, how this makes me laugh, because it wasn't but a few years later when I began to dread school. I didn't hate school; it just wasn't fun, and homework felt like the death of my soul. Alas, this cute little six-year-old version of Brittany still loved school; it was magical. Part of the magic came from the daily rides on the bus. It towered over me, with wheels that reached eye level and doors that mysteriously folded open and shut, but most importantly, it was bright and shiny like the sun. Riding the bus solidified my journey into adulthood. First stop: kindergarten; next stop: college.

But the bus and I had a rocky start. Let me explain. I can't be certain of this, but I think the first time I rode the bus was going home on the first day of school. My mom ran an at-home daycare and couldn't come pick me up from school. That was fine with me. Remember, I was practically an adult. That afternoon, when I stepped onto the bus and made my way to my seat, I burst with excitement to share with my mom all that had transpired that day. Looking around as we whipped past buildings, other cars, and people strolling along sidewalks, I realized that we were nearing my neighborhood. Time flew by, and before I knew it, the bus driver stopped and motioned it was time for me to get off. As I skipped off the bus and rounded the front of the vehicle, I waved goodbye to my new best friends. Off the bus I went. It took me a few moments to realize something didn't seem right. I looked around at the gravel parking lot where I stood and saw a long stretch of road trailing in one direction and a giant grassy field connected to a church across the way. I gathered that we hadn't quite reached my house. What's more, my mom was nowhere to be found. Fear struck me as tears welled up in my eyes. The bus driver betrayed me. I was left all alone and doomed.

After a few minutes, I composed myself and decided to walk the rest of the way home. The road in front of me looked familiar, and if I was correct, it would lead to my neighborhood and house. With one hand having to hold the strap of my backpack resting on my shoulder and the other gripping my lunch box, ready to wield it as a weapon, I took off in the direction of my home. Like Little Red Riding Hood off to her grandmother's house, I marched along the asphalt path on the lookout for sneaky wolves that may try to eat me. Halfway down the road, a car pulled up beside me and stopped. "Honey, I know you don't know me, but I live a few houses down from you; would you like me to drop you off at your home?"

Mustering up all the strength I could manage, with a shaky voice I replied, "My mom said I'm not supposed to ride in the car with strangers." The grip on my lunch box tightened, and I turned away from the lady in the black sedan and continued my journey home. *Not today, wolf. Not today.* What seemed like an eternity later, I spotted my home off in the distance, and I began the sprint of a lifetime. Pounding the pavement with each step, crossing through the grass in our side yard and up to our front door, and arms flailing like Phoebe from *Friends*, I. Made. It. Home. Though the walk probably didn't surpass a mile, I would have sworn that I had just crossed the entire contiguous United States. Dramatic much? This feat was quite heroic.

When my mom heard me barrel through the door, she came to greet me and ask me about my day. Her eagerness turned to concern when she witnessed the panic on my face. "What's wrong . . . ," but before she could finish the sentence, I started to sob. Everything that I had fought so bravely to keep down while I walked home came bursting out. A glance into her familiar, warm eyes reminded me that I was safe. My mom scooped me up and plopped me down on her lap. My body trembled, and I recounted the events that had just transpired. There had been a mix-up, like a classic scene in a comedy movie. According to my mother, the bus should have dropped me off on the corner of the street, right by my house. With the front door in sight, walking home from that spot would be a piece of cake. I think my mom gave me a slice of cake to ease my troubles. Thankfully, we never had another issue like this again.

Walking home from the bus that day, I felt abandoned, lost, and forced to walk the long road alone. It's crazy to me that even in misunderstandings, mix-ups, and lost connections, you can find yourself battling loneliness. These are moments that are not intended for harm, but they can create such damage. Then negative scripts weasel their way in and implant themselves firmly into your mind. Almost thirty years later, I found myself hearing my son talk about the same sinking feeling of loneliness, and my mama heart wasn't prepared for it.

Sitting across the table from my oldest, we talked about life after our recent move over a bowl of ramen noodles. Ethan's a lover of sushi and ramen—well actually, he's a lover of all food. That day in particular I noticed a difference in him and wanted to touch base to see how he was. As we talked, Ethan admitted to feeling lonely. That statement caught me off guard because if you knew this kid, you'd know he's like the male version of me. "Fun," "energetic," and "the life of the party" are a few phrases used to describe him. So to know he had resigned himself to finish the rest of high school alone crushed me. He continued, "It's not easy being the new person in town. Everyone already has their friend groups; they don't need anyone else."

He explained that he dreaded showing up to church on Wednesday nights. Walking in the door, he had a short window of time to scan the room looking to see if he knew anyone. On the off chance he lucked out and knew someone, he'd go stand around them trying to insert himself into the conversation. Most of the time, however, he wouldn't know anyone, leaving him to hang out in the corner alone. Banished to the Island of Misfit Toys. Like he had a neon sign flashing over his head saying, "I'm alone." To make matters worse, sometimes Ethan said he'd hide in the bathroom texting people to see if they'd show up until he had enough guts to head back into the room. My heart broke for this child, mainly because I've been there myself growing up—shoot, there have been times I've felt that way as an adult.

Loneliness will make us do crazy things. If you've found yourself hiding in bathrooms or corners trying to gather the courage to try again, I hope you see that you aren't the only one. First, let me say I am sorry. You shouldn't have to hide. Second, you are full of bravery, and I am so proud. You took a step in trying something new and finding people; that is huge. I see you. God sees you, and he has his arms wrapped around you, holding and protecting you right now, even at this moment, as we read from Psalm 91. Do you feel him? "His massive arms are wrapped around you, protecting you. You can run under his covering of majesty and hide. His arms of faithfulness are a shield keeping you from harm" (Ps. 91:4 TPT).

No matter if you're new in the town or not, you deserve to have friends. I've noticed that it's a lot easier for teens to say they are "loners" than it is to admit they're sad and they are struggling in that moment to feel seen or make friends. I get that. You feel like you're the one choosing this life rather than it being a season chosen for you. I genuinely don't believe anyone wishes to be alone. Even the most shy, introverted people want to feel like they have somebody on their side. So let me just tell you the truth, in case you need to hear it: *You don't deserve loneliness. It's a lie from the enemy.*

Our lives and days can be interesting. You truly never know what to expect. When your husband works at a church, you often find yourself there prepping and planning at odd hours during the week. Most of the time, we'd make it a family affair and have everyone go to pitch in and spend time together. This particular day proved to be no different. The kids bounced around the church gym, shot baskets, hula hooped, and raced around pretending to be superheroes. Sam and I used our precious time while they were preoccupied to set up for the service that weekend. It didn't take us long, and to celebrate our accomplishment, we decided to load up the kids and head out for ice cream cones.

The kids funneled through bathroom breaks while Sam shut everything down in the gym, and then we all packed into the van. Listening to music blare and the general chaos that comes with a large family like ours, we left for our sweet treat. However, as Sam drove out of the parking lot, he noticed some commotion in the side mirror. It was Paisley, pants to her knees, racing toward the van. We forgot Paisley! With a quick pump of the brakes, the van halted. I jumped out of the vehicle and toward Paisley, with my arms wide open ready to catch her. Full of panic and fear, this poor little girl had just been left in a dark and lonely place and then witnessed her family driving off, leaving her behind. Talk about mom guilt—I apologized profusely. Did she want cake? Pizza? A pony? Whatever it was, I would get it for her.

That's how Ethan felt when life was fun and he had an established group of friends. But then when he least expected it, the story changed. Ethan saw the life he once had gone and now he was left chasing after others, trying to find his place.

The struggle of believing you are broken and alone is not a new story to you. It's one that bleeds out across all areas of your life. Through work, your family, and friendships, there's a script that leaves you wanting more but feeling you deserve less—less joy, less community, less value. Statistics show that three out of five people actively feel lonely.[1] According to a poll on Instagram, 72 percent of people I am connected with feel alone. And we wonder why anxiety and depression are so prevalent. This script is not only damaging to your heart and mind, but loneliness can also affect your physical body negatively. Studies liken loneliness to being as damaging as smoking fifteen cigarettes a day.[2] It's more dangerous than obesity. Friends, that is serious information. We long to belong; even our bodies speak to how desperately we need to be seen and known.

When I flip through my Bible, I find many reminders stuck in between the pages, like little treasures for me to discover for another day. Most of the time, I find sweet notes from friends, drawings from my kids, or important things God taught me scribbled on little scraps of paper. But there's one treasure that wrecks me every time I come across it. My stomach drops and my throat catches with one glance. What could bring about such emotion? A folded sheet of paper with name tags pasted all over it. Each sticker holds the name of a teen I met at a conference years ago.

I travel often to speak to churches and organizations and at conferences. It's probably one of the highlights of my job. Each event leaves a little imprint on my heart, always for different reasons. This particular time was no different. Months prior I had been asked to come speak to a group of teenage girls about identity. Nothing fires me up more than being able to help a group of girls understand who they are and see how awestruck God is with them. After sharing with the entire group in the main session, I had the opportunity to speak with a smaller crowd during one of the breakout sessions. Outline in hand, exercises at the ready, I quickly felt the need to go off script. Instead, I took the time to listen and hear the pain they each carried. There was this invisible great divide between these girls and their parents. A divide that spans generations. Somewhere along the line parents and children became enemies, where secrets were kept, spies were sent out to gain intel, and plans were crafted to make life harder. Or at least that's how these girls viewed things. Tucked in a room, down the hall, these girls found safety in that space, in my presence, and began to share their pain and heartbreak. The weight of their words crushed me. Though I have spoken to thousands of women and teens, in that moment I felt completely helpless and not equipped to help them. But I was determined to try.

One thing became clear to me: this invisible divide between them and their parents left them feeling lonely and isolated. After everyone had a turn to share, the room grew quiet. I had each of them take out a piece of paper to write a letter to their parents. The prompt? "What I wish you knew." I could see the fear in their eyes, but I reassured them no one else would see the letters. To ease their fears a little more, I joked that they could rip them up and throw the pieces in the trash, put them in an envelope I brought and planned to take home, or even eat them. I didn't care, I just wanted them to understand that this was their chance to get all the thoughts, hurts, and feelings off their chests. And boy did they. After writing for a few minutes, I placed a trash can in the middle of the room so they could tear their paper up. Some shredded their pieces so tiny it looked about the size of cupcake sprinkles. Others asked to send their pieces home with me in my envelope because they feared their words might be found in the trash can. Then one girl tossed some pieces in the trash can, tucked some in my envelope, and to my horror, placed one specific shred in her mouth and swallowed. What could have been so bad that this sweet fifteen-year-old felt she needed to eat the paper her pain was written on? Driving home that day, I wept. Because for the first time, I felt that I did absolutely no good. These girls were struggling, hurting, and lost in lies, and they felt alone in them. But they're not. This is a lie from Satan. I need you to know this now. You don't have to navigate these teenage years alone. You have adults in your life wanting to walk alongside you and help you. There is no war; we are waving our white flag in surrender. Trust me on this. Here's my challenge to you. It's my way to help you begin to heal this relationship with your parents and the adults in your life. I want you to write a letter to them.

- What do you wish your parents (or adults) knew? I want you to find a safe space—in your room, closet, wherever—grab a clean sheet of paper, and write a letter to your parents. Once this is done, tear it up and throw away the pieces (however you feel comfortable doing so).

The negative scripts being fed to you by the enemy will keep you stuck in your loneliness. *There is something wrong with you. Nobody wants to be your friend. You are hard to love, handle, and so on.* But this is what I know, a truth spoken of in God's Word: "It is not good for . . . man to be alone" (Gen. 2:18 NLT). From the foundations of the earth, one thing is true: God did not create man to be alone. To believe differently is to believe a lie. And that is what I chose to cling to.

Are you sitting here, holding this book, and feeling stuck in a lonely season? I want better for you. And I can confidently say that God wants more for us as well. Paul writes in the book of Romans to assure the Christians in Rome of one paramount thing: "No power in the sky above or in the earth below—indeed, nothing in all creation will ever be able to separate us from the love of God that is revealed in Christ Jesus our Lord" (Rom. 8:39 NLT). Today, we are going to believe that nothing can separate us from God's love, and that means he won't leave us alone. This comforts me, as I hope it does you. This also means that we can work to flip the script in our minds, a script that holds us back from community with others, because we are loved, always and forever, fully and completely. Now let's get to work.

- Have you ever felt lonely? Do you maybe feel lonely right now? Share a little bit about that below.

_____

_____

_____

_____

_____

- Let's write down the negative scripts that come to mind when we think about loneliness and the stories we wrote above.

_____

_____

_____

_____

_____

Notes

1 Susan Perry, "3 in 5 American Adults Report Feeling Lonely, and Younger Adults Feel It the Most, Survey Finds," *MinnPost*, January 31, 2020, https://www.minnpost.com/second -opinion/2020/01/3-in-5-american-adults-report-feeling -lonely-and-younger-adults-feel-it-the-most-survey-finds/.

2 "The Loneliness Epidemic," Health Resources and Services Administration, https://www.hrsa.gov/enews/past-issues/ 2019/january-17/loneliness-epidemic.

No power in the
sky above or in the earth
below—indeed, nothing
in all creation will ever
be able to separate us
from the love of God
that is revealed in Christ
Jesus our Lord.

—

ROMANS 8:39 NLT

eight
NEW SCRIPT
I Am Never Alone

I t's a Thursday night, and I find myself on my hands and knees with a damp towel and a hot iron in hand with a YouTube video tutorial blaring. "What am I doing?" you may wonder. Burning my fingers. That's what I'm doing. Also, I was trying tirelessly to dissolve red wax from my white carpet. When we moved into this house, I knew the white carpet would prove to be a problem from the start, but what I didn't expect was a game night gone wrong.

We had been playing a rousing game of Throw Throw Burrito, and the cards indicated a duel between my two youngest girls. They lined up, back-to-back, as you do in any good duel. Squishy burritos in hand, we counted down from three as they took steps in opposite directions. "One." They spun around and chucked the Mexican cuisine at each other. The goal: hit your competitor before they get you first. Only one flying burrito went rogue, tossing and turning until it smacked a lit Christmas candle perched on a table. The force tossed the candle to the ground, and bright-red wax flew everywhere. We froze in silence and tried to process the events that had transpired. The wood floors, white walls, and white carpet resembled a gruesome crime scene. It's forever known as the Great Candle Massacre of 2021. The view overwhelmed me, and even though I was unclear about how to tackle the mess, I started in a small section and kept moving on.

If you were to ask the kids what surprised them most about this ordeal, they would unanimously say that I kept calm the entire time.

And people think miracles don't happen. After we wrapped up cleaning, we were left with a speckled red pattern on the carpet, a faint Jackson Pollock for all to see as they entered our home. In years and homes past, this would have sent my anxiety through the roof. I couldn't imagine inviting people over with such an atrocity. However, in this house and new chapter, it didn't faze me much. The splatter seemed like a fitting symbol for the chaos of our year. Plus, we didn't have people to invite over who could gawk at our mess. We were alone.

Months later, attempting to flip the script on my negative thoughts, I invited some women to my house. I pulled the trigger on the invite before I had a chance to back out. It was a good thing too. Because that Thursday night, on the floor, ironing my carpet, I regretted putting myself out there. What if I tried to meet people again and it flopped? *Why can't I make friends? Why is this so hard?*

The truth is, even though I know community is vital, I also know it can be hard to build at first. But I also know that anything worth having is hard. It's showing up when you feel like you don't belong. It's putting in the time to open up and be vulnerable. It's getting to know others and their stories. It's not easy, and it's not quick. But it's real, deep, and hard-fought. That is beautiful.

Emma was a thirteen-year-old girl, full of spunk and excitement, and had the sweetest British accent in the world. After a series of emails with her mom, I had the chance to talk a little with Emma. We spoke of her life in England as well as the similarities to and differences from life in the United States. Then she shared with me about an exciting new school she had recently been accepted to, one that required her to leave her family for long periods of time but that was full of great opportunities. After a few months there she was enjoying the school but struggling to find friends. Emma wanted to know what was wrong with her and why she didn't fit in. I could see the sadness in her eyes as she went on to explain how girls can be mean and how isolating it feels to be away from her family.

During our video chat, my dog burst into my office, and our conversation took a fun turn to our pets. We talked about how crazy our dogs were and how much they loved food. In fact, Emma spoke about her dog's obsession with bacon—so much so that they can get him to follow whatever command given if they have bacon nearby. As we went on talking about bacon, an idea hit me: "Emma, that's what you need to do. You need to bring the bacon!" By the look on her face, it was clear I had confused her. She was a great person and would make a fantastic friend, but these girls (as are most girls her age) were focused on themselves and other things. Not in a bad way; it was just easier for them to see the things right in front of them, easily missing the new girl in need of a friend. So Emma needed to entice them with *bacon*: "Your job over the next two weeks is to pursue and initiate time with three friends you'd like to be close to. Remember, this is the building phase: the more time you put in, the better. Make the choice to believe they want to be your friend—none of it is rejection." Excited to try out our new process, we ended our call, and I waited to hear back two weeks later. Wouldn't you know, Emma said it worked. When she took the time to pursue the friends, they were actually really sweet and excited to get to know Emma. They couldn't believe she felt alone and didn't mean to make her feel that way. Way to *bring the bacon*!

Why is it so hard to find friends? The answer is simple. When it comes to community, we expect it to simply drop in our laps. We yearn for the girl we met at church or school to text us and make things happen. But when she doesn't, we are left deflated and crushed. This pain leads us to believe the negative script playing in our mind—*she doesn't like me* or *something's wrong with me*. Swallowing these lies as truth, we find ourselves feeling alone, isolated, devastated, and defeated.

Why do we demand that others pursue us while not taking any of the responsibility ourselves? Why can't we take the risk and try first? I'm convinced that true community lies on the other side of your comfort zone. We can't continue to listen to the scripts that lead us to believe we are only worth loneliness. So let me tell you like I told Emma; it's time for you to *bring the bacon.*

I mentioned my oldest, Ethan, in the last chapter, but I didn't get to finish the story. Here's what you need to know. A few months after our sad ramen dinner, Ethan expressed interest in joining the wrestling team at school. This sport was new to our family, and honestly, I didn't know what to expect. But Sam and I could see light in his eyes as he talked about his newfound passion, and we wanted to fan that flame as much as we could. He spent hours practicing, watching YouTube videos to learn techniques, and getting all the necessary gear. A few days out from his first match, I ordered giant three-foot cardboard cutouts of his head to bring with us. We were his people and we would be loud and proud with our support. What we were surprised to see was a handful of other people from our church who came to cheer Ethan on as well. They heard about his meet and wanted to see him. This kid, who not long before felt like he had no one, really had a loud and passionate group in his corner, so he was never alone. We are there to challenge, encourage, and hold him up as he navigates life. Side note: Ethan is actually quite good at this wrestling thing. But even better than that, he's having a blast and making great friendships with his team.

We often hear the story from Exodus of when Moses commanded God's people to fight the Amalekites. Moses stood atop a hill and watched as God's army fought while he held a staff high above his head. As long as the staff remained lifted, God's army would win: "As long as Moses held up the staff in his hand, the Israelites had the advantage. But whenever he dropped his hand, the Amalekites gained the advantage" (Exod. 17:11 NLT). But soon, Moses's arms got tired. That's when his two right-hand men, Aaron and Hur, stepped in. Seeing the struggle of their leader, mentor, and friend compelled them to action. They each grabbed one of Moses's arms and held it up until the battle was won: "Moses' arms soon became so tired he could no longer hold them up. So Aaron and Hur found a stone for him to sit on. Then they stood on each side of Moses, holding up his hands. So his hands held steady until sunset" (Exod. 17:12 NLT). Because of Aaron and Hur, the Israelites won the battle.

Interestingly enough, before this battle, we read about Moses using his staff to perform miracles two other times. First, facing certain death and no way of escape, he stretched his arm and staff out to part the Red Sea and rescued the Israelites from Pharaoh (Exod. 14:16, 21–22). Shortly after, in the wilderness, Moses struck a rock to create a spring of water (Exod. 17:5–7). In both of these cases, Moses could succeed alone. But the third time was different; he needed the help of others. He needed his friends to jump in. All alone, he would fail.

What if they simply stood in the back and cheered Moses on? What if they merely grabbed their best set of fig leaf branches and, with killer moves, chanted, "Moses, Moses, he's our man; if he can't do it, no one can!" But they didn't. Thank goodness for that. Scripture doesn't tell us if Moses asked for help or if his buddies were proactive. Either way, they noticed their friend struggling and stepped in. They didn't try to take over, condemn him for his weakness, or seek out their own glory. They knew that when he won, they all won.

There are times in my life when I feel like Moses, holding up my staff, trying to balance life and family and all the challenges they bring. It doesn't take long before my arms burn and shake, begging for release. That's when my bowl girls step in. They are my Aaron and Hur. They hold up my arms when I no longer can so I can win my battles and so God can be glorified. The best part is, I get to be Aaron and Hur for them too. Frankly, that's one of the greatest honors of my life.

I recently heard about a study that took place in the 1990s.[1] Now, I'm not the scientific type; things like this aren't my go-to choice of reading materials. But this one struck a chord with me. Let me explain. Scientists created the Biosphere 2 project, three acres enclosed beneath a giant glass and metal dome. They hoped to study the earth's living systems all in one location. During the study, the scientists discovered something surprising. Trees grew rapidly inside the bubble, more so than outside in their original environments. However, they fell over before fully maturing. This baffled the scientists, who took a closer look. After observing the outer layers of bark and root systems, they realized that the lack of wind inside the dome was a problem. It was affecting the overall stress grading of the trees. If you're like me, you have never thought about the stress grading of wood or lumber. But what the scientists found was that ordinary wind helps trees solidly grow and absorb the sun properly. The bubble and "optimal" growing environment handicapped the trees. They could not thrive and grow to their full potential without stress.

We can learn much from this study. It's funny how God's creation can intertwine; things that apply to trees can even find truth in our lives. Hiding in a bubble, alone and safe from others and the outside world, can only help you to a point. It won't be long before you fall over. The stress, struggles, and challenges of life are never pleasant, but they become bearable when we have people to help carry the load. The more we invest in the idea of community, the more we get vulnerable and let others in, and the more we do life together, the deeper and stronger our roots get. These roots matter. We need to build roots down deep with people so that we can withstand the stress and wind of this world. Other people help us fight the harmful narrative that we are alone in our struggles. But we must also grow our roots down deep into the Word of God. Which of these scripts do you need most?

- Old script: *I am broken and all alone.* New script: *God has promised to never fail or abandon me* (Deut. 31:8).

- Old script: *I can't trust anyone.* New script: *Because the Lord forgave me, I can forgive others* (Col. 3:13).

- Old script: *People are bothered by my struggles.* New script: *I am not a bother; God calls for others to share in my burdens* (Gal. 6:2).

- Old script: *My friends and family have rejected me.* New script: *God says that he is a Father to the fatherless and a defender of widows and that he places the lonely in families. I am loved, fought for, and belong* (Ps. 6:5–6).

👑 It's Time for Your Glow Up!

What are some scripts you need to flip? Below, write them out and ask God to help you flip them. You can also look through your Bible, maybe google verses dealing with this topic, or even ask trusted friends, family, or leaders to help you.

Old Script: _____

New Script: _____

Old Script: _____

New Script: _____

Old Script: _____

New Script: _____

Grab a Hug

This may sound silly, but it's the best thing you can do for yourself. Christy Kane, a clinical mental health counselor, teaches about the power of an eight-second hug. Did you know hugs are powerful? They are. Technology, including cell phones, is changing the makeup of our brains. It's negatively affecting our mood and overall well-being. One key component in helping combat this is physical touch. When you hug for extended periods, say, for eight seconds, your body relaxes into it and releases the hormone oxytocin. Kane states that you need eight eight-second hugs every day. This is proof that human touch and connection are vital parts of our makeup.

I once spoke at a youth event where I introduced the idea of needing eight eight-second hugs a day. I explained in depth about the benefits to your emotions and mood when you get those hugs. Then I had them all stand up and hug another person in the room as we counted for eight seconds. Giggling erupted as they held their embrace for the whole time. Later in the day, I heard of girls going up to cute boys saying, "Brittany said we need eight hugs and I still need five more." This made me chuckle. Leave it to middle school girls to figure out how to work the system in their favor. Either way, I want to encourage you to do the same. Try it: put down the book, and find a friend to embrace you for eight seconds right now. (I'll wait.)

- List your eight hugs below:

_____

_____

_____

_____

_____

_____

_____

👑 Find Your People

I understand that this statement feels obvious, but don't tune me out. We expect people and friendships to drop in our lap, but most of the time that isn't how it works. Often it requires us to be the first to make a move. I want you to be brave for a second. Is there a person you've met that you'd like to get to know better? Don't wait for them to reach out to you. Call them. It may take a few attempts, but stick with it. What if genuine friendship were just around the corner? (I'm here for you too. You can find my phone number and email in the back of this book. For real, reach out.)

- Who have you always wanted to reach out to but have been nervous to do so? Write their name below, then set a goal to contact them this week.

_____

_____

_____

_____

👑 Get Plugged In

Want to find an easy way to accomplish finding your people? Get plugged into a local church or club at your school. Dive in, and find a place to connect. In many of these places you can jump in and serve others. Like at church, you can volunteer with younger kids, helping them have fun and feel seen. Then while you're helping others, you are building community with the people around you. I've found that when I take my eyes off myself and focus on helping someone else, my mood shifts. I see things differently and ultimately discover that I am not alone. I'm a part of one big family. Find your family.

- Are there any clubs at school you're a part of? Are there any you would like to join?

_____

_____

_____

_____

_____

- Do you go to church? If so, where can you get plugged into and start serving?

_____

_____

_____

_____

_____

Work Your Rhythms

I've noticed the times I feel the loneliest and defeated are the times I am not operating in healthy rhythms for myself. I bet this resonates with you too. But the term *healthy rhythms* has become a buzz phrase, one that everyone uses and one that most don't understand how to use or implement. I don't want to complicate things or confuse you, so let me show you what a healthy rhythm looks like for me.

I start by creating a good work-home-life balance with healthy boundaries. Each day, this means waking up before my children, grabbing a cup of coffee, and spending time in silence before God. As busy people, we tend to run from silence, but often, it's exactly what we need. Let the Lord speak into your silence. I read my Bible and have worship music constantly playing. A big objective for me is self-care. The Bible says that your body is a temple (1 Cor. 6:19–20)—love it, respect it, and care for it. Lastly, I move my body.

Nothing changes your mood more than getting up and allowing your blood to pump through you. Running is my jam. It calms me, resets my mind, and makes me feel alive. There are days when I feel the loneliness creep in, and the best way I know to combat this feeling is to reset. I may run, nap (I'm pretty sure there is nothing a good nap can't solve), or relax my body.

Take a seat. Rest your arms on your legs, and close your eyes. Focus on slow, deep breaths in and out. Then begin taking inventory of your body. With each body part, from the top of your head to the tips of your toes, release any tension you may be holding on to. Section by section, feel your body give way and relax. This is a game-changer.

For a generation that is extremely connected, we have never felt so alone. Do you want to know why? It's because of our phones. These handheld devices can never replace face-to-face time. We try hard to, but it's not, nor will it ever be, the same. The problem is that when we try to substitute our screens for in-person connection, we become more and more isolated and depressed. Then we hurt even worse because we were not created to do that. Now put down your phone and find your people. Don't let loneliness have the final say or be the label you wear. There is a community out there for you. God promises for us to "have life and have it abundantly" (John 10:10 ESV). Believe him, and flip the narrative in your mind. I'm here fighting with and for you.

Note

1 Anupum Pant, "The Role of Wind in a Tree's Life," Awesci— Science Everyday, accessed March 1, 2022, http://awesci.com/ the-role-of-wind-in-a-trees-life/.

glow up
DECLARATION

You are never alone.
You are worthy of a life
full of beautiful friendships
and community.
And you're sought after
by a God who
craves time with you.
The companion and friend
who will never leave.
You were created to have a bestie
and be a bestie. Now get out there
and find your people.

"Most daring" was a title given to me in high school by the senior class. A title that didn't necessarily seem fitting in the moment but a role I'd gladly step into. For me, trying the new, crazy, scary thing felt like a fun challenge to conquer. *WHY NOT DO ALL THE THINGS?!* I realize now this isn't everyone's thought process, and for that, I'm sorry. Just kidding; the world doesn't need to be full of daredevils.

It's funny now thinking about it, because I can definitely understand where they came up with this idea. As a kid in middle school, I rode the bus daily. Yes, I know, this sounds about as glorious as it was. Anyway, our ride to the school only had a few students and a grumpy but lovable driver—we'll call him Bob—whose buttons I regularly pushed. Really, he loved me, but I pressed the limits with my behavior because I was the teacher's (I mean bus driver's) pet. One day, Bus Driver Bob made my energetic classmate and myself sit in the front rows. Probably a good choice, since the day prior we got into trouble for lying across the tops of the seats while dancing the Macarena. Why did we do this? I guess to see if we could. See, pushed the limits. Let me just say, the moves get a little tricky while navigating the winding streets to school. Either way, our sweet bus driver didn't make a big fuss, and we teased him that the only reason he made us sit up front was because he liked chatting with us.

It didn't take long before my friend and I got ourselves into some mischief. I can't be certain on whose idea this was, but I leaned over to Bus Driver Bob's seat belt and quickly clicked the release. It flailed around, smacking him in the chest as it retracted to the base. We hid behind our seats and snickered at what just happened. "Oohhh, Brittany! Don't do that!" Bus Driver Bob yelled as the veins pulsed in his neck and his eyes grew three sizes. He grabbed his seat belt and forcibly clicked it across his lap. After a minute or two, I had the bright idea of repeating my new party trick. So I reached over and clicked the release. Again, the seat belt flailed like those inflatable figures advertising outside of businesses. The mischievous joy this brought us caused us to laugh uncontrollably. "Oohhh, Brittany! You better not do that again!" This time Bus Driver Bob's cheeks were flush, much like the red light we were stopped at. But being the daredevil that I am, I decided to call his bluff and test my luck once more. I enjoyed the game too much. Without weighing the odds or really thinking about what I was doing, I leaned over once more, clicked the release button, and laughed as the free-flowing seat belt ran amok. However, this time things were different; I could feel the tension as the "cheese wagon" grew silent. I had crossed a line, and he was angry. When we pulled up to school, Bus Driver Bob asked me to stay back. My friends laughed and teased me with "You're in trouble" as they walked on to class, and I waited to see what happened next. Bus Driver Bob pulled out a clipboard and began to fill out the paper on it as he discussed his disappointment in my actions. Apparently, you can't torture the driver without getting kicked off the bus. Something about it not being safe. Oops.

This was my attempt to win the crowd, get a laugh, and make friends. However, my plan backfired, and I not only got in so much trouble, but I ended up alone and the butt of a joke with my peers: "Don't pull a Brittany!" or "Brittany's so dumb, did you hear what she did?" Have you ever taken things too far? Pressed the limits, pushed the boundaries, only to fail miserably like me? There was a lesson to be learned in this, but all I could do was to beat myself up. Why didn't I know when to stop? In an instant, my whole middle school life became cloaked in shame. I had worked so hard to give the appearance of a "good girl," but now I was just the troublemaker. People wouldn't look at me the same. What would teachers think? My youth pastor? *You're such a screw-up. You're not a good Christian girl; nobody will listen to you now. You can't be trusted. You're a mess; you should be ashamed.* Negative scripts are tricky because some are birthed through the stories and moments that you would least expect, and then others are from simple childish mistakes. Shame is one of the biggest culprits. Here's what you need to know: Satan is a wordsmith. He has a way of twisting thoughts, ideas, and memories into shameful scripts we read as truth. Sometimes even the silliest of mix-ups turn into embarrassingly shameful ones.

We've talked earlier in the book about how boys never looked at me and saw a girlfriend, just a buddy to hang out with. Well one year I had the chance to attend a homeschool prom with some friends of mine. Was I homeschooled? No, but my friends from church were, and my parents thought this prom option seemed safer than the one I could attend at my public high school. My mom and I shopped for dresses and planned out makeup and hairstyles, but we lacked one thing. I needed a date to this event. Boys my age in ninth grade appeared annoying and childish, at least in comparison to the cute senior in our church youth group. His friend planned to attend the prom with my friend, so it only seemed natural for me to ask him to be my date. To my surprise, he agreed to go, and I about died. *THIS CUTE SENIOR IS TAKING ME TO PROM.* Play it cool, Brittany, play it cool. On the night of the prom, however, I learned that I do *not* know how to play it cool.

The girls all gathered at my friend's house, turning it into a beauty salon, as we primped for our magical night. An eternity later, we were dressed and ready as the boys arrived to pick us up and pose for pictures. My cute senior pulled up to the house in his father's vintage Corvette, which his dad graciously let him borrow for the night. Is this a dream? He whisked me away, and off we went to prom. After the less-than-exciting dance, we headed to a local fast-food restaurant to grab some ice cream and change out of our formal attire. As the group sat talking in a booth, I headed out to the Corvette with clear instructions on how to pop the trunk so I could put my stuff in. Unfortunately, by the time I made it to the car, I had forgotten everything he told me. Maybe I should have paid better attention to his words instead of planning our wedding in my head. Too embarrassed to walk back in and admit my childlike dreaming, making me feel like the young/dumb kid, I began to pull, push, and grab every button, lever, and handle in that car—because I could just figure it out, right? Why did cars have to be so complicated? Why are there so many buttons, levers, and handles? After minutes of trying, I located the right lever. The trunk popped and victory was mine. *Or so I thought.* With a smirk on my face and a pep in my step, I marched back into the restaurant and tossed the keys back to my cute senior. *Way to go, Brittany. This is how you play it cool. You're nailing this.*

Getting back into the car as we headed out to play Putt-Putt, the cute senior put the keys in the ignition and turned the car on. Lights flashed all over the dashboard with warnings this ninth-grade nondriver couldn't comprehend but caused my cute senior's eyes to almost explode as they opened wide. "Did you do such-and-such?" he asked. *(Still to this day, I don't remember the words he asked. I was too busy turning fifteen shades of red while I plotted my immediate escape.)* "No, I just opened the trunk to put my stuff in. Just like you instructed me." *Cool, I just lied to the cute senior.* The words, my lie, flew out of my lips at lightning speed. My heart pounded in my chest like it was auditioning for our high school drumline. And I knew in this moment I looked like an ignorant kid and not a girl older, wiser, and worthy to date this cutie. I wanted desperately to impress him, but instead I might have just broken his car. We went back and forth as I played ignorant to the problem and he tried to figure out what happened, especially since he and I were the only people to touch the car. *(See, I didn't think this through. He knew he didn't mess up the car, so the only logical choice was me. And yet, I held to my lie because I couldn't look foolish.)* Thankfully, the cute senior was able to undo all the flashing lights I caused to go off, with no damage to his dad's car, but not without a short freak-out session.

Believe it or not, we were able to have fun the rest of the night, and I thought I might have turned things around. *Maybe I have a chance with this guy?* That was until the car ride home. We talked and recalled all the fun from our night, but at some point during a break in our conversation, I fell asleep. Yes, I fell asleep on a date with the cute senior. Like a child on a long car ride, I passed out in the passenger side of a vintage Corvette. "Hey, we're at your house." The words that awoke me as we pulled into the driveway of my home. Completely humiliated, I mumbled a quick goodbye, gathered my things, then scurried up the sidewalk and into my house, slamming the door behind me. With my face pressed against the front door, I looked to make sure the cute senior left, and I prayed for death to rescue me from this embarrassment. How could I ever show my face around church again? I was so ashamed and was certain I'd never live this down. *This is why you don't have a boyfriend. No boy will ever like you. Everyone will know about this; you'll be the joke of the church youth group.*

That night ranks high on some of the most embarrassing moments of my teenage years. I swore for years to take that secret to the grave. Now as an adult, it doesn't seem so bad, and I laugh just thinking about it. While this story was silly and humiliating, I know the feeling of shame and wanting to tell no one, ever. But holding these secrets full of shame will only hurt you. Even at your age, they will eat you alive. Worse than that, these scripts will act as building blocks to a foundation of shame as you grow.

Here's the thing about shame: it hides in the dark and is locked up where no one can see but is fully capable of keeping you arrested and silent. What if this was the enemy's plan all along? It was and is. Satan works day and night to convince you that it's OK to make the wrong choice. He gives you permission, and somehow those choices don't appear that grand, gross, or scary. It's amazing, really. He's patient, deliberate, and shrewd. This has been the story of man since Adam and Eve in the book of Genesis:

> The serpent was the shrewdest of all the wild animals the LORD God had made. One day he asked the woman, "Did God really say you must not eat the fruit from any of the trees in the garden?"
>
> "Of course we may eat fruit from the trees in the garden," the woman replied. "It's only the fruit from the tree in the middle of the garden that we are not allowed to eat. God said, 'You must not eat it or even touch it; if you do, you will die.'"
>
> "You won't die!" the serpent replied to the woman. "God knows that your eyes will be opened as soon as you eat it, and you will be like God, knowing both good and evil."
>
> The woman was convinced. She saw that the tree was beautiful and its fruit looked delicious, and she wanted the wisdom it would give her. So she took some of the fruit and ate it. Then she gave some to her husband, who was with her, and he ate it too. (Gen. 3:1–6 NLT)

With one lie, we are putty in his hands. Then he flips the script on you and feeds you lines of disgust, disappointment, and shame. *How could you? You are the scum of the earth. People will reject you if they find out.* We believe him because we know what right and wrong are. Deep in our guts, we understand our mistakes. However, the shame is Satan's special twist on the truth. He's a professional, and he has practiced since the creation of the world: "At that moment their eyes were opened, and they suddenly felt shame at their nakedness. So they sewed fig leaves together to cover themselves" (Gen. 3:7 NLT). Like Adam and Eve, we let shame take hold, and we cover ourselves to hide the secret.

Do you know what I'm talking about? The shameful secrets you have to keep tucked down deep in your heart, never to see the light of day? It's in the darkness we lose because that's where Satan has all the power. As adults we often assume kids your age can't understand such pain and darkness. But here's the thing: Satan can turn any scenario into something that feels so deep, dark, and heavy. He makes you believe that the adults around you—who are there to help, love, and support you—are in fact there to judge, punish, and torture you. I know this because believe it or not, I was a teen once. Never did I want to share my mess-ups, struggles, or pains with others. *Would they think less of me? Would I fail them? Would they be ashamed of me?* In my gut I knew they would, so I kept quiet.

Sitting on the floor in my office, cracking jokes about the latest fashion trends I didn't comprehend, I sensed Julie had more to say. She flipped her phone like she was tossing a coin, weighing with each flip whether she would share or hold it in. *Heads I spill the tea, tails I keep it in.* The tension climbed with each turn until I threw my hand over the phone and pinned it to the floor. "Just say it," I said. "Whatever it is, speak it out loud." Her eyes met mine, uncertain of how I knew there was anything to share and fearful of what might come if she did speak up.

"I've messed up so bad," Julie shared, almost as if to reassure me that I didn't want to know. "It's OK," I said. "No matter what it is, I still love you." We sat there for a minute in silence, eyes locked on each other until her secret bubbled to the surface.

For months, Julie had been sending sexy selfies and nude pics through Snapchat. That wasn't her original goal for being on the app. The filters were fun, her friends were on it, and wasn't it what all the other kids were doing? But then some guys, most of them whom she knew, began asking for pictures. At first, she declined. *Were they crazy?* A part of her felt flattered, though. Somebody liked her, someone noticed her. As time passed, she found herself flirting with these guys and laughed off each attempt they tried to get her to send a compromising picture. One day, however, a guy persuaded her to snap a quick photo. He reminded her it would be gone in a second, nobody would know, and it would be fun. If she was honest, the secrecy seemed exciting, and the idea of a guy pursuing her felt nice. So she did it. Before she knew it, one photo with one guy became multiple photos with multiple guys.

Julie looked away as tears rolled down her cheeks. The weight of guilt and shame crushed her. She was stuck in this loop and couldn't see a way out. If she ever refused to send a photo to one of the guys, he threatened to expose her. The idea of that proved too much for her to bear; she needed to keep him quiet, so the cycle continued. "I can't stop," she told me. "My life is ruined." I grabbed Julie and held her tight, crying at the weight of what she shared. A bright and beautiful young girl stared into a dark void that she thought was her future. How could an eighteen-year-old feel there was no hope, that she had damaged things beyond repair?

It's not just Julie; shame is a much too common theme among the teenagers I meet. Girls living their lives completely blocked from what God has for them because they believe harmful scripts and cannot see the way out. Most of the narratives they believed are too painful to speak. Because of them I have seen teenagers create the most intricate disappearing acts, rivaling even the greatest magicians, in efforts to hide the truth. But once it's hidden, in the silence, they suffer.

Freedom from secrets can appear scary. I get it; really, I do. But how is hiding in shame working out for you? For most of the girls I coach, including Julie, it's not. Instead, they live in constant fear, guilt, and the crippling weight of what they hide. They aren't winning; they're dying inside. I heard a quote the other night while Sam and I binge-watched Netflix before bed. It was from *Call the Midwife*, and as I heard the words, I sat up with purpose, proclaiming, "This is it! This is what I want these girls to know!" Maybe this can become an anthem for your heart; it's time to speak up:

> Secrets can maim us. Shame can close us off. What we bury drags us down, and there can be no flight from it. Speak. Speak up. Speak out. Find the words to express the facts that matter. Bring them out into the light, into the air. Hiding heals nothing. Silence saves no one. When we are heard we can be acknowledged. When we are known we can belong. Bound together we are stronger and braver than we know. Alone we are fragile and at the mercy of the storm.[1]

When the secret is given power, we will lose it every time. But what if we speak what we are afraid to utter? What if we bring what is in the darkness into the light? Where there is light, darkness cannot be. It's a simple fact. Walk into a dark room and turn on a flashlight; instantly, the darkness dissipates as far as the powerful ray of light shines. The apostle John referred to Jesus as the light when he wrote, "The light shines in the darkness, and the darkness can never extinguish it" (John 1:5 NLT). How do we win over the darkness of the shame spoken over our hearts? We bring the light of Jesus, and we watch the darkness run.

- What are some moments in your life when you have felt full of shame? Write them out.

- Let's write down the negative scripts that come to mind when we think about shame and the answers we wrote above.

_____

_____

_____

_____

_____

Note

1 *Call the Midwife*, season 10, episode 6, directed by Afia Nkrumah, aired May 23, 2021, on BBC1.

The light shines
in the darkness,
and the
darkness can
never
extinguish it.

—

JOHN 1:5 NLT

ten

NEW SCRIPT

I Am Not Ashamed

The notification popped up on my phone with an email from a familiar name. The subject line read, "Thank you." A smile filled my face as I remembered my chat with Riley weeks prior. She had walked up to me with her foster mom one Sunday and asked to talk. Her mom said that she specifically wanted to speak with the pink-haired lady because she thought if anyone would understand and not judge her, she would. She guessed right.

In a muffled voice with her chin tucked into her chest, Riley shared with me about her life. She always worked so hard to be the person people loved, doing whatever it took for people to like her. She couldn't bear the thought of someone, even a friend, rejecting her because that's what her parents did. "I don't know if I believe all of this stuff. I don't know if God is real," she blurted out in an effort to change the conversation. Riley was hiding a deep, dark secret.

The year before, she found herself friends with a guy who was a little older than her. He quickly became her best friend, and they did everything together. From binge-watching the Harry Potter series to Putt-Putt and trips to Target, they were inseparable. But not long into the friendship, the guy began to ask Riley to cross physical lines she didn't feel comfortable with. At first she could dodge the requests by redirecting the conversation; unfortunately, that didn't last long. Her friend then threatened to leave her and spread lies about her as he left. This crushed Riley, and she ultimately agreed to the demands. Crossing these lines with this "friend" made her feel gross, and she couldn't tell anyone. What would they think about a fourteen-year-old doing such things? This continued until, in her lowest moment, she came close to ending her life. Through the help of the Lord and good people like her foster parents, Riley was working to make it to the other side. Now troubled with guilt and shame, she found herself talking to me. The story left me speechless. It didn't surprise me that this girl struggled to believe in church or God at all. My heart broke; so much trauma in such a small life, this couldn't be the end of her story.

Tears rolled down my cheeks as I leaned in looking Riley straight in the eyes: "I think God wants me to say, 'I'm so sorry this happened to you.' This wasn't his plan, and he definitely doesn't want you to carry the weight of this shame." Sometimes people just need to hear an "I'm sorry" because often in the mess of trying to fix things, we forget that simple yet powerful phrase. We forget to see them as a person, broken and sad. They need to feel seen and not like they're a project to be completed.

I have an incredible friend named Jenny who founded a ministry called Our Daughter's House. ODH, as we call it, exists to help rewrite the futures of girls aging out of the foster-care system. These girls, or their daughters, get to have a family, learn life skills, and get ready for adulthood. Each one is loved, cherished, and known. Jenny and her team care more for the individual than the label, case file, and so on. During an interview, Jenny once said, "People don't need to be rescued; they need to belong." Those words sent chills down my spine. So much wisdom and truth. That's what Riley needed from me in the halls of our church. She didn't need a rescuer; she needed to feel like she belonged. And that was something I wanted to make sure she heard.

God was working to free Riley from the chains of things that had happened to her and choices she had made. The weight of her past kept her hidden and fearful to move forward in life and even trust other people. The step she took that day to share her truth with me felt monumental and incredible. Like John reminds us, "They overcame him by the blood of the Lamb and by the word of their testimony" (Rev. 12:11 NKJV). I knew that God would continue to make her whole as she shared her story in safe places. Even more than that, I knew he would work to make good come from it. Her story, her past, no matter how painful, could be used to remind others they are not alone. She could hold the keys to their future. *That* was power and nothing to be ashamed of. That was the truth I called up and out of her. As we talked, we focused on ways to rewrite the negative scripts in Riley's heart. In her email to me, she wrote, "Thank you for speaking with me last week. I feel so much lighter and I can't explain it. For the first time in a long time, I'm happy."

The lighter feeling Riley wrote of? Freedom. That broken, fragile girl no longer existed, and a beautifully redeemed one stood in her place. A switch flipped in her life when she called out the scary, dark parts. She recognized the lies of the enemy, who planted such hurtful and damaging scripts. She then brought them to light and shined truth on them, which led to her bravely stepping out into freedom.

Her freedom from shame is contagious. Shelley Giglio, a women's pastor at Passion City Church in Georgia, once wrote on Instagram, "It's very hard to tame a free woman," and I couldn't agree more. There's no taming Riley; she is free and on a mission. And what a gift to have this fire at such a young age. This is my prayer for you too—that you would call out the shame you hide and bring it to light, allowing God, his Word, and safe friends to help you change the harmful scripts that you believe. Maybe even right now, at this moment, could you be brave enough to believe that God can heal you and make you free? Could you speak this out loud in faith? I'll do it with you: *I believe you can free me!*

You see, like Riley, I too have been broken into so many pieces that I began to question whether God just needed to throw me away. *What good was I anymore?* In the dark and shameful places, those are the words that scream the loudest. Because our flaws are fatal, right?

That's what our society teaches us. If it's broken, throw it away and replace it with something new. We load the curbs with broken, discarded junk on trash days—cracked chairs, shattered dishes, and unrepaired toys all prepared to meet the green truck of doom because the owner decided they no longer had value. It's the proverbial hall of shame for every neighborhood.

Have you seen *Toy Story 3*? You might want to go ahead and grab a tissue. Near the end of the third movie, Woody and his gang find themselves in a garbage dump where they narrowly escape toy doom a few times. Each time, relief meets their faces as they believe the battle is done, until the next round comes. Finally, they see a light. But to their dismay, this isn't the light to freedom; it's the light of a fiery incinerator. The toys begin scaling the trash heap and try to move farther and farther away from the flames, which proves unsuccessful. Jessie essentially yells out, *Buzz, what are we going to do?* Seeing the terror in Jessie's face, Buzz gathers his thoughts and silently reaches for her hand. They know the time has come. One by one, each toy grabs the other's hand, and the scene ends in a deep and crushing moment with Buzz and Woody locking eyes. The music swells as the toys tearfully clench their eyes and cling to their friends. The end is near, and they accept their fate. I watched the movie when it first came out, and the theater filled with sniffles, "oh nos," and shock as an animated children's movie brought us to tears. (You may never throw anything away again after watching this.)

Do you know that broken and shattered feeling? You've just assumed the trash is the best place for you. You've accepted your fate. But this doesn't have to be your future. The amazing news is that God sees us differently. He loves to take us, broken hearts and all, and make them whole. Just like in the movie, a last-second escape can be yours if you are willing to let those cracks show.

I once read about a pottery process developed in Japan over four hundred years ago. It's called *kintsugi*, the art of embracing damage. These artists take broken ceramic pieces, restore them, and seal them back together. But instead of hiding the cracks or flaws, they trace them with brilliantly shining gold paint to highlight their mended parts. After all is said and done, those once dump-worthy pieces of pottery are now stronger and worth way more money than when they were first created.

The same can be said about God; he is the ultimate *kintsugi* artist. He sent his son, Jesus, into a dump-worthy world to redeem and restore us. Because of this, we don't have to live alone, unequipped, or broken. Instead, he wants to take those hard places, those broken pieces, all those sins, and restore us and let us shine so we will be worth so much more than we ever were before.

Let me ask you again. Are you broken? Are you hiding in the shameful scripts you believe? Look around at the broken pieces of your heart, and slowly pick up each dark sliver and hold it up to the brilliance of his light. Because, friend, you need to see some truth outshine that shame, truth about who God is and who you are in him, knowing that only "In Your light we see light" (Ps. 36:9 NASB). It will possibly be one of the hardest, bravest things you've ever done, but you are worth it. Also, can I just say this? There is beauty in you and in your brokenness, not later when you're "fixed" or after your life moves on and things get better, but right now, in the brokenness, there is beauty. You are worthy of love, right here, right now.

A huge part of overcoming the script of shame is learning to find biblical hope. God is the ultimate hope-giver and turns everything painful into something beautiful if you're willing to be a part of it. Speaking of pain, try being Israel, a nation chosen by God, stuck in exile and captive to the Babylonians, a group of people known for their harsh ways and ungodly behavior. The Jews struggled to follow and obey God. Many attempts were made to convince the people of God to turn away from the sin they were in and return but to no avail.

Sometimes we find ourselves in exiles of our own because of the choices we've made. Before you know it, all hope appears lost, and your future is grim. That was the Jewish people. The prophet Jeremiah called out to the Jews while they were in exile, and boy, did he say a lot, but not many listened. Frankly, Jeremiah was one of the most unsuccessful prophets, according to the world's standards. People didn't listen to him, others fought against him, he didn't have any wealth, and by all criteria, he flopped. But that's not how things are measured in the Kingdom of God. Jeremiah had a job to do—speak truth to God's people—and that's exactly what he did. He met people in the midst of struggle and loss, and he wanted desperately for them to heed to God's words and find hope. He was a good man.

Jeremiah 29:11 says, "'For I know the plans I have for you,' declares the LORD, 'plans to prosper you and not to harm you, plans to give you hope and a future.'" Most people stop at the end of this verse, assuming their life will be wrapped up in a neat little bow. I mean, it does make a great decorative sign or pillow, but I'm afraid we miss the point in this passage if we do so. There is power when we keep reading. Looking a bit farther, it says,

> "Then you will call on me and come and pray to me, and I will listen to you. You will seek me and find me when you seek me with all your heart. I will be found by you," declares the LORD, "and will bring you back from captivity. I will gather you from all the nations and places where I have banished you," declares the LORD, "and will bring you back to the place from which I carried you into exile." (Jer. 29:12–14)

These people were broken, were lost in exile, and needed hope. And the Lord said, *This is how you'll get it. Call on me, seek me with your whole heart, and I will bring you back. I will restore those cracks.*

Can I echo the prophet Jeremiah for a second? Come to the Father. He is calling you, showing you what you need to do and how to heal, and reminding you that he has a beautiful plan for your life. Your past, no matter how painful, can truly be one of your biggest gifts for the future. Your story can help shine the light for the person next to you who may find themselves shattered in pieces of their own. Not long ago, I heard this quote from Bill Johnson, and it plays in my mind as negative scripts try to take hold of my mind. I think you need it too, bestie. "Any area of your life that has no hope is under the influence of a lie." Try trading your old scripts, which lack hope, for new ones:

- Old script: *I am ashamed of my mistakes.* New script: *Because of what Jesus did for me, I know there is no condemnation for those who are in Christ* (Rom. 8:1–2).

- Old script: *Because of my past, God can't use me.* New script: *God promises to help me do his will and not live in disgrace* (Isa. 50:7).

- Old script: *I have done wrong; therefore, I am wrong.* New script: *I am a fully accepted and beloved child of God* (Rom. 8:15–16).

- Old script: *I am a broken mess.* New script: *God is doing a good work in me and is faithful to continue working in and with me* (Phil. 1:6).

⸛⸜⸛ It's Time for Your Glow Up!

What are some scripts you need to flip? Below, write them out and ask God to help you flip them. You can also look through your Bible, maybe google verses dealing with this topic, or even ask trusted friends, family, or leaders to help you.

Old Script: _____

New Script: _____

Old Script: _____

New Script: _____

Old Script: _____

New Script: _____

Love is the biggest and best way to fight shame and flip the script. Nothing spells out love like the truth of God's Word. As you work through these new scripts, speak them over your life, and walk them out each day, I need you to remember the biggest factor fighting against your freedom—the desire to hide. Shame grows in secrecy, silence, and the fear of judgment. It can hold you hostage while taking your life and your potential for ransom. But it doesn't have to. Satan wants you to live in that shame, but Jesus wants so much more for you. Fighting shame takes some work, vulnerability, and being honest with where you're at. The following are a few practical ways for you to break the silence and begin to shift your thinking.

Find the Chair

When you notice negative thoughts, feelings, or even tensions rise up in your body, you need to stop and listen. Let me use this analogy to explain. Your life is a table, and each chair at the table is a different piece of you—a little girl, a curious teen, a young mom, and so on. Each seat holds a different season of life, including struggles, trauma, and more. But each chair is worthy and valid, and each chair needs a spot at your table. It's all part of your story. But often, when one version of you finds herself standing and screaming in her chair, crying out to be noticed, you don't pay attention or give her attention. You shut her up, trying to silence and hide what is really going on. Instead, why don't we recognize her, see what she says, where she's been triggered, and perhaps even the harmful script she's believing. Only then can she be helped. (Shout-out to a friend for this analogy.) One of my dearest friends once told me that her younger self needed a hug and to know she wasn't alone. You better believe I grabbed and pulled her in tight and whispered the truth to her lies.

Share Your Story; Be Real and Honest

When you speak, others feel seen and understand that they aren't the only ones struggling. Giving it words will help you awaken and leave the shame behind. Trust me—when you share your story in safe places, fear, guilt, and shame lose power. How do you find safe places? Find a few people who you think might fit the bill, and then try it out with small things. If it goes well, great. Open up more. If it tanks horribly, I'm sorry, but I need you to be brave and try again. Your people are out there, and they are ready and waiting to help you flip the script on shame.

- Who are three people you could feel safe enough to share pieces of your story with? Can you be brave enough to tell them this?

_____

_____

_____

_____

_____

⚜ Listen and Love

If you have been trusted with someone's story, don't try to fix the problem, and don't share your growth points or anything of the sort. Just sit and love. Let the person sharing feel like they belong and are beautiful, in that moment, as they are (because they are). They aren't beautiful *when* things are fixed; they are so incredibly loved right then and there. They are an image bearer of God. Show them that.

- Who are some friends who share their stories with you? How can you better listen to and love them?

_____

_____

_____

_____

_____

⚜ Shine a Light

Don't hide behind mistakes or toxic scripts. The secrecy causes you to become trapped even further. Speak the truth, and shine a light in the darkness. The light I'm speaking of is God. What does his Word say? Are there things you need to confess and get off your chest? Drop the weight, and cling onto forgiveness. The Bible says that when we confess (or tell the truth about a situation) to God, it brings forgiveness. But there's another type of confessing; the Bible says that when you confess to others, it brings healing. And there is freedom and hope in Christ Jesus. It's yours for the taking. There is forgiveness and healing in confessing. Now grab a friend to speak this over you, or let me speak it: "Therefore, there is now no condemnation for those who are in Christ Jesus" (Rom. 8:1).

- Write this down as you speak it out loud:

Therefore, there is now no condemnation for those who are in Christ Jesus.

You can take these steps to walk in freedom. It's time to drop the shame, bestie. Speak up because your life is worth it. Let me leave you with this truth written by David as he praised God in the book of Psalms: "You've gone into my future to prepare the way, and in kindness you follow behind me to spare me from the harm of my past. You have laid your hand on me!" (Ps. 139:5 TPT). Take heart; the Lord has gone ahead and prepared a way for your future. It's not ruined, it's not over, there is still hope. At the same time, he follows behind you to protect you from the harm of your past. You have the freedom to move forward without shame, without hiding, without hesitation. Let him redeem the negative scripts that broke you.

glow up
DECLARATION

You are not bound by shame.

No story, struggle,

or hidden past can weigh you down.

At your very core,

you belong as a

precious daughter of God.

You are not broken; instead,

your gold pieces will shine brightly

for all to see.

Freedom is yours for the taking.

Now stand tall and

show others the way.

eleven

OVERALL SCRIPT

I Can Shine

Have you ever soaked in the sun? No, I don't mean the conventional, laying out to tan in the summer kind of way. I'm referring to the moment when you're outside and you turn facing the sun with your eyes closed and head tilted up. Anytime I'm outside and can catch the sun on my cheeks, I stop and take a minute. Running on a trail, among the trees and nature, I'll stop, turn, and soak it in. Walking into work, I'll stop, turn, and soak it in. Stepping out to check the mail, I'll stop, turn, and soak it in. No matter the action, I always pause for a moment in the sun. There's something about it for me. It's beyond the heat and warmth. Instead, when the sun shines on my cheeks, it feels like a kiss from God. Like a brief meeting between him and me when he tells me I'm his favorite. Like the verse written in Isaiah played out in real life, "Arise! Shine! Your light has come; the LORD's glory has shone upon you" (Isa. 60:1 CEB).

As time passes, the beauty of moments like those increases. On hard days and good days, I can go outside and simply soak in his presence. I can rise and shine. These are "glory moments," little pockets of memories when I could nearly feel the tangible presence of God on me—so personal and precious but compelling me to continue on and, in turn, shine for others to see. Do you have "glory moments" too?

Moses sure did. In the book of Exodus, Moses was tasked with the job of leading the Hebrew people to the promised land. This came on the heels of their newfound freedom from Pharaoh and the Egyptians. But before Moses made any big moves, he wanted to make sure the Lord would go with him. He knew being in the Lord's favor and presence was the only way they could make it. After a back-and-forth between Moses and God, Moses asked for God to show his glory to him. There, on top of Mount Sinai, God tucked Moses in the cleft of a rock and passed in front of him, allowing Moses to get a glimpse of God's glory. Immediately, Moses dropped to his knees and worshiped God. For the next forty days, he stayed on top of the mountain with the Lord. When Moses came down the mountain after receiving the Ten Commandments, the Bible says he was literally shining: "He wasn't aware that his face had become radiant because he had spoken to the LORD" (Exod. 34:29 NLT). He spent time with God, and he glowed because of it.

Now, it's easy to see this beautiful moment between God and Moses and forget all the others that brought him to that encounter. His story is similar to ours. Did he have wonderful glory moments? Yes. But he also faced struggles, struggles much like you and I have been working through in this book. Let me walk you through them for a second.

Failure and Shame

The book of Exodus opens with fear. Pharaoh feared the Hebrew people, who grew in numbers and, in his mind, threatened his reign. His fear forced him to turn God's chosen people into slaves while also instructing his people to kill all newborn baby boys. Moses was born during this strong Egyptian oppression, and Moses's mother feared for his life and hid him in a basket, which she placed, with Moses inside, in the Nile River. I cannot imagine the desperation of his mother, but her bravery allowed God to work. In the Nile one day, an Egyptian princess found the baby and ultimately rescued him and adopted him into her family. As Moses grew, he found himself caught between two worlds: one of Egyptian royalty and the other of an enslaved Hebrew people. The tension came to a head one day when Moses witnessed the cruel beatings and hard work his people were forced to endure. In the heat of passion, Moses killed an Egyptian and then quickly tried to hide his body in the sand. But like I tell my children, the truth will always surface, no matter how deep you bury it. Sure enough, the same is true in this story: "Then Moses was afraid, thinking, 'Everyone knows what I did'" (Exod. 2:14 NLT). His life now in danger for a second time, Moses fled the land.

I don't know about you, but I'd say that killing a man would qualify as a failure. This is no *Oops, I ran a red light*. It's murder. In feeling shame from his mistake, Moses did the only thing he knew to do: run. He ran from the consequences, he ran from the people he had failed, and he ran to hide in isolation. Sound familiar? We have all sat in the aftermath of our failures and hidden in shame. But the thing I want you to see here is not the mess; it's what comes next. That wasn't the end of Moses's story. Actually, it was the beginning. God didn't look down at him and think, *Why did I save your life as a baby for you to ruin it at such a young age?* Quite the opposite, my friends. God turned Moses's failures and shame into something that he would ultimately get the glory for. Just like with Moses, your mistakes don't have to be the end.

Worth and Comparison

Years later on a mountainside, Moses heard a plan from God, and it was a crazy one. God spoke to him through a burning bush. Honestly, if I heard the voice of God come from a blazing piece of shrubbery, I'd freak. Moses didn't bat an eyelash. Instead, he stepped closer and talked to God. What a guy. The time had come for God to send rescue to his people, and he wanted to use Moses to lead the way. But Moses questioned God by highlighting all his shortcomings: "Moses pleaded with the LORD, 'O Lord, I'm not very good with words. I never have been, and I'm not now, even though you have spoken to me. I get tongue-tied, and my words get tangled'" (Exod. 4:10 NLT). He didn't understand why God would want to use him to do such a mighty task. He didn't feel worthy, and he felt that his skills were lacking in comparison to others'. In fact, Moses pleaded with God to send anyone other than him. He didn't doubt God's desire to rescue his people; he just thought God chose the wrong guy.

Like Moses, it's easy to measure and weigh our shortcomings against the directions God calls us to. We're quick to shut him down, believing we aren't worthy enough, especially compared to the next girl. *Thanks, but no thanks, God. Your plans are great, I'm here for the freedom, but I think you have the wrong girl.* What if God had a purpose in asking Moses? I believe he did. What if he has a purpose for you? I believe there is one.

It took some convincing, but with his brother Aaron by his side, Moses did free the Jews from Pharaoh. God had been faithful and had gone before Moses to prepare the way. But what did Moses *do* with all God's people? Like that awkward moment at an event when the host has run out of things to do and the attendees look around, unsure of how to proceed, Moses needed a plan. After years of glory moments and seeing God's hand through every step, he knew where to turn. That's where we meet him in Exodus 34, seeking God for guidance and wisdom. After each encounter with God, Moses's face glowed with such radiance. Can you imagine? Spending time in the presence of God changes things. It changes you. Moses is proof of this. So too are we once we have fully realized our worth and laid that foundation. When we seek the face of God and the truth of his word, we understand how to shine. That light will then spill out onto everything we do and those around us. This doesn't mean you'll never struggle. Flipping the script may be a lifelong task, and reinforcing the truth consistently is a habit. Like

Moses, you can keep going back to the source. Negative thoughts won't dominate your mind and consume your identity once you've learned how to flip the scripts of your life. Your worth has been decided. Now shine like it.

One day not long ago, I found myself in a slump. I was just stuck in a rut of comparison, struggles with worth, and feelings of complete failure. A smorgasbord of emotions overwhelmed me and made me want to wave my white flag and crawl back into bed. Denying the sheets that beckoned for me, I attempted something new. The following day, I had a trip booked, and I began to think about how many other people I'd encounter who might resonate with how I felt. What if I could help flip the script for them and make them smile, leaving them better than I found them? And that's when I concocted a plan: creating Bestie Bags.

Never have I ever had so much fun creating those silly little things. Filled with candy, a Bestie bracelet, and a card full of confetti *(Are we even surprised by now?)*, the bags were designed to add a bit of joy while I met new people and learned a little about their lives. The cards weren't anything special or extravagant, just a little encouragement reassuring them they were doing a good job and that I was proud of them for showing up today. At the end of the note, I reminded the reader to shine bright, with a reference to Matthew 5:14–16:

> Here's another way to put it: You're here to be light, bringing out the God-colors in the world. God is not a secret to be kept. We're going public with this, as public as a city on a hill. If I make you light-bearers, you don't think I'm going to hide you under a bucket, do you? I'm putting you on a light stand. Now that I've put you there on a hilltop, on a light stand—shine!

Keep open house; be generous with your lives. By opening up to others, you'll prompt people to open up with God, this generous Father in heaven. (*The Message*)

This is probably one of my favorite verses of all time. How cool to think that we each have the ability to bring out the "God-colors" in this world! We have been crafted to shine in such a way that reflects him and his glory. But we can't hide the light he's given us. Did you see that part? It doesn't make sense to spend time in the Word, learning how to flip our scripts, and begin to shine, only to hide. No, we need to stand tall and shine bright so others can see. They need help too. They need to see you shining so they understand it's possible, so they have the courage to try, so they know hope is not lost.

Have you ever taken a second to look at a prism? The transparent cut and shaped glass figure holds a beauty of its own. I have one hanging in my office, and while I enjoy the fun aesthetic it brings to the space, my favorite moment happens when the sunlight hits the prism at the right angle. Because once the light hits the prism, it refracts and shines in other directions. You can often catch a beautiful rainbow glowing across the room—a perfect light of blues, reds, and yellows, God-colors shining for all to see. It's mesmerizing. The light can't stop from shining and refracting off the prism, and within an instant, it becomes involuntary. You are like this prism when you work to fix the damaging scripts taking hold of your life and allow the light of Christ to change you. Soon, his light shining in you begins to refract off of you, and you can't help but create the most incredible God-colors for all to see. You become mesmerizing because you allow God's light to shine. It's not your light; it's his light shining within you. This is the light others need to see.

"I'm so excited for tomorrow!" You may be asking me, "Well, what's tomorrow?" I'm glad you asked. (Not that you had a choice, ha!) My daughter was talking with this lady at church. They were asking each other very basic, acquaintance-type questions when all of a sudden, my daughter interjected, "I'm so excited for tomorrow!" to which the lady asked, "What's tomorrow?" And my daughter replied, "A brand-new day!" This caught the lady off guard, probably like it did you as well in this moment. But you see, that conversation stuck with that lady. So much so that later in the evening when she was home talking with her son she found herself saying, "I'm so excited for tomorrow!" to which her son then asked, "Why?" And she grinned as her face lit up when she said, "It's a brand-new day!" A few days later, the lady saw me at work, and she told me this entire story and how it's literally shifted her mindset. Now she's excited for the new day. All from a little encounter with a teenager she didn't know but who was shining bright for all to see.

How can one conversation alter your mood and change your day? Because your light, even if through just a smile or a simple word, has power. Your light shines and causes darkness to shatter. Through the work of the Holy Spirit, you have been gifted with this light. The more you embrace his light and allow it to shine through, the more the effort becomes involuntary. Even the tiniest of actions can break through the dark spaces in someone's heart and let a little hope in. Try it.

And when you really need help brightening someone else's day, or even your own, try this chant/song I came across on Instagram but have adopted as my own. In fact, I've been known to dance around the house creating the most embarrassing moves while singing this to my children. Within minutes, we're in a better mood. (Pro tip: the crazier the dance moves, the faster the mood shift.)

Today's gonna be a good day, gonna be a good day.
Today's gonna be a good day, gonna be a good day.
Get the negativity outta my face, I want positivity in my space.
Today's gonna be a good day, gonna be a good day.
I hope you have a good day, have a good day.
I hope you have a good day, have a good day.
Get the negativity outta your face, you want positivity in your
    space.
I hope you have a good day!

Throughout this entire book, I've given you scripts to assist you in flipping from the old negative scripts to new statements of truth found in the Bible. Now I want to give you statements to remind you to shine. We're going to call them Shine Scripts, simple reminders to shine. You're lucky—I came close to calling them Sparkle and Shine Scripts, but I figured not everyone is as extra as I am. Girl, I am guacamole-at-Chipotle extra—and if you don't know of the wonder that is Chipotle, first of all, I am so sorry, you have been wronged, and second, that is an extreme amount of extra. So for your sake, we'll go with Shine Scripts.

- Shine Script: *The glory of the Lord shines on me so I can rise and shine* (Isa. 60:1–2).

- Shine Script: *I was created to shine brightly for others to see* (Matt. 5:15–16).

- Shine Script: *When I share the hope and love of Jesus, I shine like the stars in the sky* (Dan. 12:3).

- Shine Script: *The light of Christ is in me and helping me shine and producing what is good, right, and true* (Eph. 5:8–9).

👑 It's Time for Your Glow Up!

What are some other Shine Scripts you can add to this list? Below, ask God to show you ways that you can shine. Then look through your Bible, maybe google verses, or even ask trusted friends, family, or leaders to help you complete them with Scripture.

- Shine Script: _____

- Shine Script: _____

- Shine Script: _____

Everything you read in the Bible is yours for the taking. Here's the deal: some of us choose just to read it, and some of us choose to believe it. Don't just read these words; they are yours for the taking. Believe the truth they hold, and let these words change you. Now is the time for you to shine, free and clear from the damaging scripts. Let me implore you as Paul did to the body of believers in Ephesus. Both of you faced a crossroads. Will you allow darkness to come in and affect how you live, breathe, and ultimately shine? Will you be persuaded in the ways of culture and the world, or will you remember the truth of God's Word? So I say to you, "Awake, O sleeper, rise up from the dead, and Christ will give you light" (Eph. 5:14 NLT).

Bestie, rise and shine.

You're here
to be light,
bringing
out the
God-colors
in the world.

—

MATTHEW 5:14 *The Message*

twelve

A few years ago, I hosted a women's event at a church. The night was full of worship, fun, and a plea for women to rediscover their worth in Christ. There was a stack of pipe cleaners for the women to create crowns to wear at each table. It was something simple and fun, but it was a reminder of the fact that they are daughters of the king of kings. We had a blast, and the women bought into the theme. It's nice to let loose, have a little fun, and relive the dress-up princess days from childhood. We lose that as we grow. Suddenly, life becomes a series of trials, stressors, and breaking points. The joys of play, princesses, and belief in good tend to fade. But that night, women found themselves believing once again.

One beautiful face in the crowd was a girl named Shantel. Her presence commanded attention, and her name echoed the sparkle and sass she possessed. As I passed by her table while she engaged the women around her in a rousing tale, I stopped to meet this firecracker. It didn't take long for me to realize that Shantel is the quintessential life of the party and someone everyone desires to have in their circle, myself included. She is quick to let you know what's on her mind and is eager to fight for those who need it. Everyone needs a Shantel in their lives. We became fast friends as we talked, and I discovered that she taught at a local elementary school. Even more exciting, she had started a program at her school, Project Beauty, for the girls in her grade. The more she shared, the more this girl amazed me.

She created Project Beauty for girls to learn how to be girls, grow in their self-confidence, and have a positive mentor to guide them on the right path. Shantel shared with me that she dealt with bullying throughout her school years and that the bullying worsened in high school. That's when she pictured what it would have looked like to have something like Project Beauty in place for her. At the same time, Shantel began hearing her fourth graders talk about their struggles with their insecurities and even about life-ending thoughts. It broke her heart to hear how young they were while feeling these feelings, and she decided she needed to do something about it. Her goal was simple yet powerful: to make sure those girls felt loved, supported, and empowered to take on anything they may face in life. Her life had been shaped by struggle and hardships with bullying, but she didn't let those harmful moments and damaging scripts rule her life. Instead, Shantel dug deep to see what might have helped her through those years, and then she became that for other girls, girls who struggled in silence but desperately needed someone to come alongside them and show them the way. She found purpose through her pain by channeling her energy to help those girls. I wanted to be like her when I grew up. What an inspiration; what a powerhouse.

Shantel's face beamed as she spoke of her proudest moments: when two sisters, who initially couldn't stand being around each other, were able to bond and grow in their relationship, and when a parent came up to thank Shantel for teaching her daughter how to advocate for herself not only in the classroom but also with others. "This program is my entire heart," she said. What a strong role model speaking life and hope into the lives of these little girls. Shantel fought to help them flip the damaging scripts already playing in their minds, and then she worked to show them how to rewrite the narrative. A generation was getting a fresh start, all because a teacher, once broken, stepped up to make a change.

I love Shantel's story because she didn't wait for someone to give her permission to do this. She didn't seek to make grand plans in hopes of fame, global reach, or anything fancy like that. Do I believe her idea is genius? You bet. But Shantel didn't consume herself with those thoughts. She simply stepped in and offered what she had (experiences, lessons, etc.) in hopes of changing just one life. It would be worth it all to change even one life. Thankfully, she has shaped the lives of many, which is not surprising in the least. Shantel is a world changer, and I am honored to call her a friend. What can you do, in your life right now, to make a difference like Shantel did?

It's one thing to live a life of freedom, but it's another to lead people to the same freedom. A few nights ago I sat around my living room and listened to the stories of high schoolers and their young adult leaders. Do you want to know the common thread in the discussion? Mental health. Each one of these stories I listened to involved a personal struggle with self-harming thoughts or others very close to them who have taken their own lives. In my house, on my couch, right in front of me. Did you know that suicide is the second leading cause of death in fifteen- to twenty-four-year-olds? THE SECOND. The statistics are astonishing. Right now a generation, your generation, is hurting. They are stuck in negative scripts, leaving them lost and feeling hopeless. It's in the faces of those we pass on the street or in class at school. The neighbors we wave to, friends we share meals with, and those who live under our own roof. It's in the brightest faces in a room and the quiet thinkers sitting off to the side. Friends, the pain and suffering is all around us. We have the opportunity to do something about this, to reframe the narrative of our culture and this generation. Right now, you have the power through the Holy Spirit to help bring change. You can make a difference in the lives around you just like Shantel did. Help them flip their scripts and find hope. This world is desperate for it.

In the Bible, we read about four friends who were desperate for their friend to receive help. What troubled the friend? He was paralyzed. These friends heard of a man named Jesus and of miracles he performed. Full of faith, they carried their friend to a home in Capernaum where Jesus taught. But when they arrived, the four friends were faced with a problem: "They couldn't bring him to Jesus because of the crowd, so they dug a hole through the roof above his head. Then they lowered the man on his mat, right down in front of Jesus. Seeing their faith, Jesus said to the paralyzed man, 'My child, your sins are forgiven'" (Mark 2:4–5 NLT). Nothing would stop these men from bringing their friend to Jesus. Their passion and faith compelled Jesus to speak. Through the power of words, his words, we see what happens next: "Then Jesus turned to the paralyzed man and said, 'Stand up, pick up your mat, and go home!' And the man jumped up, grabbed his mat, and walked out through the stunned onlookers. They were all amazed and praised God, exclaiming, 'We've never seen anything like this before!'" (Mark 2:10–12 NLT). These men didn't struggle to walk, and they were free to move around. But that freedom didn't satisfy them; they dreamed of the same freedom for their friend. Will we have faith like that for our people? Enough faith to show them the way, bring them to Jesus, and help them flip their scripts? Can we be like these men who stopped looking at themselves and saw the needs of others? Their freedom is counting on it.

In sharing this story from Mark, I skimmed over a few verses in the middle. Let's get back to that. After Jesus saw the man lying on the floor in front of him, he said, "My child, your sins are forgiven" (Mark 2:5 NLT). I wonder about the reaction of the onlookers. Did they understand what Jesus spoke? Did they mock or question the presence of this lame man disrupting the room? Was his desperation laughable to them? I'm not sure, but in my experience, not everyone will be excited for you. Not everyone will understand. Often, through that lack of understanding or spite, they will speak words that tear you down. In this case, we see a glimpse of the reactions in the following verse:

> But some of the teachers of religious law who were sitting there thought to themselves, "What is he saying? This is blasphemy! Only God can forgive sins!"
>
> Jesus knew immediately what they were thinking, so he asked them, "Why do you question this in your hearts? Is it easier to say to the paralyzed man 'Your sins are forgiven,' or 'Stand up, pick up your mat, and walk'? So I will prove to you that the Son of Man has the authority on earth to forgive sins." (Mark 2:6–10 NLT)

What if the paralyzed man had listened to the questioning of the crowd or the Pharisees? What if the interaction between them and Jesus had made the paralyzed man nervous? What if he thought that his friends were acting foolishly? Then filled with humility and fear, this man might have allowed the words of others to create a barrier between him and his healing—between him and his freedom—all from bitter men who lacked understanding. We see it often in Scripture, instances similar to the rantings of Pharisees who acted in fear and spoke bold words that proved untrue and caused damage. Our words and actions hold power—how will you use them? I would be remiss to not point out that doubt, criticism, and even suffering ended at the feet of Jesus. When you fight to flip the script in your mind, whether from words of your own or those of others, they are no match for God's Word. Bring them to the feet of Jesus, and watch him silence the critics and tell you to pick up your mat and walk.

I never got to meet those friends written about in the Bible—because obviously I'm not that old. But I wished I could have sat and talked with them for a little while to really see what caring for people looked like. There are few people I've met in my life who remind me how to love people like these friends did. Ava is one of them: a middle school powerhouse, full of spunk, perseverance, and heart. Running was one of Ava's passions, and her first year on the track team she worked hard, improving leaps and bounds above everyone else. Did this mean she was the fastest in the field? No. Did that stop her from showing up and trying her hardest? No.

One particular track meet, Ava had been scheduled to run three back-to-back events. Never had she done that before, but eager to prove her abilities to the coach and herself, she agreed. After finishing one heat, she would run to change her numbers, take a sip of water, and then race back to the field. Not a chance to rest in between. Taking the field for her third event, she nearly missed it all together as she rushed to switch out shoes for cleats. This set a panic in her heart as she choked back tears, feeling like she let everyone down, herself included. The gun sounded, and off she went, racing the hurdles, her least favorite and most troublesome of all the events. Ava didn't place, but she also didn't finish last. Passing the finish line, she collapsed, exhausted and defeated, disappointed with her time.

But then Ava did something magical. She picked her body up off the grass and walked over to her teammate. This girl, new to the team and the event, finished after Ava in last place. Learning the hurdles is a process and a scary one at that. Ava understood this and wanted to encourage the teammate and not let her feel defeated even a little bit. Why does this matter? Because Ava stopped focusing on herself and turned her eyes to the people next to her. She got out of her head and cared more for others than her own time and success. That girl is my hero.

I learned a lot from Ava that day. Here's what I need you to know; adults are watching you. While most of your life has been spent watching us, seeing what we do and how we handle things, we also watch you, learning *from* you. Seeing how you handle things encourages us to show up, not give up, and in this case, care about others. Let me encourage you with Timothy's words, "Don't let anyone think less of you because you are young. Be an example to all believers in what you say, in the way you live, in your love, your faith, and your purity" (1 Tim. 4:12 NLT). You have power right now in this season even at your age. That I can promise you.

Can I tell you a secret? Lean in real close. Sometimes you have to be your own hype girl and jump in to be proactive for the moments when remembering truth seems to be difficult. I know this because my husband taught me. Like the friends fighting to bring their struggling friend to the feet of Jesus, he constantly looks for ways to remind me of God's Word. Sam has always held the title of my biggest supporter, and he knows exactly how to keep me moving forward when I feel defeated. Who knew a life coach would be so good at encouraging others and yet struggle to remember things for herself? Well, it's true. *Cue face-palm.*

A few years ago, I sat on the floor in a hotel hallway telling my husband about the crazy revelation God had just given me: "I'm supposed to champion women to freedom!" Never had anything seemed so clear to me, and at that moment, nothing could stop me. A passion burned so deeply in my soul for these women and their freedom. It was an Esther moment, for sure.

But before I could say another word, Sam interrupted me: "Brittany, maybe you should take a second while you're on this high and film a video coaching yourself for the moments you doubt. This process could take a while, and you need to remember what God said to you today." What? I didn't need a video of me talking to myself, but I humored him and filmed one anyway. Can I tell you something? He was right! (Please don't tell him.) There have been many times during this book journey when I've questioned what God spoke to me during that retreat. My memory gets distorted by time, fear, and discouragement. But in those moments, I know where to go: back to my video. That Brittany was unstoppable in the things God had called her to. She didn't know exactly where the path would lead, but she charged forward by boldly believing God. Her unapologetic belief and passion ignite a fire in me all over again each time I watch. These were the words to myself; by now, I can quote them by heart:

> Brittany, I wanted to encourage you tonight as you're sitting here in a hotel, reeling from the few days that you've gotten to spend at this coaching retreat. I wanted to take a second and film this in case at this moment you are questioning what God has said. He has confirmed over and over again that you are meant to speak to women; you are meant to bring them freedom. So remember the verse Esther 4:14. Brittany, God has called you for this purpose. And if you don't stand up and do that, he's going to bring someone else along to do it instead. Then you will miss the blessings from it. Who knows, maybe you were created for such a time as this. Remember who you're passionate about and what happens if you don't. So don't be fearful; fight for "her." OK? Believe it.

Maybe Sam was onto something. Maybe the best thing you can do is to record yourself in the moments when you hear God so clearly, when a breakthrough comes and you find yourself shining bright. With this light, you become your own hype girl.

Queen Esther is one of my favorite characters in the Bible. She displayed such wisdom, courage, and strength throughout her life. I love bold, aggressive moments of bravery, like William Wallace of real-life and *Braveheart* fame exhibited. We're not surprised by this at all, are we? But sometimes, quiet, feminine strength can be beautiful. Esther's story does this well. At the beginning of the book of Esther, King Xerxes finds himself looking for another queen. Apparently, the last queen embarrassed him during a royal party, and in his anger, he decided to banish and humiliate her. Yikes. In his search for a new queen, he sent his servants to find the most beautiful and talented women to choose from. Esther found herself among the few, thanks to her wisdom and favor. King Xerxes became smitten with Esther: "And the king loved Esther more than any of the other young women. He was so delighted with her that he set the royal crown on her head and declared her queen" (Esther 2:17 NLT). During her reign as queen, her cousin Mordecai rose in status, enabling him to work near her at the castle. Through his wisdom, he warned Esther before she became queen to keep quiet about her nationality and their relation to one another. When Mordecai angered Haman, a prideful leader and right-hand man to the king, by refusing to bow to him, a plot was crafted to annihilate him and the Jewish people. Esther feared for her life as well as for the lives of her people. How could their fate be spared? But even through the deceit and threats brought on by Haman, Esther showed wisdom and strength. She leaned on the truth and guidance of those she trusted, those who helped keep her mind and heart at peace.

As the threat of death neared, Mordecai implored Esther to rise up and fight for the Jewish people, her people: "For if you remain silent at this time, relief and deliverance for the Jews will arise from another place, but you and your father's family will perish. And who knows but that you have come to your royal position for such a time as this?" (Esther 4:14). Esther had a choice. Would she give way to the fear and the negative scripts in her mind? Or would she listen to her cousin? He had a plan to help her. He knew God would protect her, and he knew she wouldn't be alone. Her choice would free a generation of people or lead to their massacre. As scary as it all seemed, the power was in her hands. Mordecai wanted her to see that God had positioned her for just this time and that he could be trusted with their futures. Mordecai knew the truth and fought to help Esther to see it. What if your role in helping others flip their scripts could impact a generation? What if you could be the Mordecai to someone's Esther? What if you hold the power, through what you've learned, to take part in helping someone else shape and change the world? Spoiler alert: you do, and you can.

Let me be Mordecai to you for a second. I took the well-known verse in chapter 4 of Esther and adapted it a little to help you. This is my attempt to call you into action, just as Mordecai did to Esther. While you probably aren't freeing the Jewish people from imminent death, you can help bring freedom from harmful thought patterns that can be just as damaging. I want to invite you into this script. Let's call it a little charge or encouragement over you as you help others fight for their freedom. For me, it helps to write down statements or verses that I want to remember on cards and stick them in places I pass by throughout my day. I'd like to encourage you to do the same.

> _____ (Your Name Here),
> God has called you to rise up and help a generation flip
> their scripts. And if you don't stand up and do that,
> he's going to bring someone else along to do it instead.
> Then you will miss the blessings from it. Who knows?
> Maybe you were created for such a time as this.

Look around you. Who else needs this message? Others in your life are watching you and looking to you for help, consciously or not. Inevitably, helping others is what this book has been about: to help set them free, to help them shine and rewrite their stories. People everywhere are missing out on abundant life and are underutilizing their God-given gifts because they've given into these negative scripts. They are drowning, and they're looking for help.

Once a friend was introducing me, and she said, "Brittany is like a sparkler in the hands of God." Never had I heard anything like that before, but I loved the way it sounded and consider it one of the greatest compliments anyone has ever given me. How cool is it to picture yourself as a beautiful, mesmerizing sparkler, being lit and directed by the very God who created you. I'm not sure whether I'm worthy of such words, but I hope to live up to them. You can be a sparkler too. You have done the work of flipping your script. With your glow up, you light the way for those around you, and you can train others to do the same. I don't want to do this alone—can we do it together?

Who knows?
Maybe you were
created for such a
time as this!

—

ESTHER 4:14

conclusion

BENEDICTION

Glow Up

M any years ago when I only had two children the age of toddlers, I was featured in *Parenting* magazine. While you may not be familiar with the publication, it was a big deal, back in the day. What about me might have been deemed worthy of being printed on their pages for hundreds of thousands of people across the globe to see? A little story about my boys. Doesn't sound too exciting, does it? Hold please.

One morning I woke up a little later than usual, thinking how grateful I was that my boys had slept in, giving me extra rest. When I walked into their shared bedroom, I was shocked to see neither of them there. Confused and stunned, especially since one of those tiny tots still slept in a crib, I shook my head and went down the hall to see where they were. I'm assuming you aren't a parent yet, but rule number one in parenting: if the house is quiet, mischief is happening. It's almost a guarantee, and this case is no different. Nearing the kitchen, I heard a tiny voice say, "Oh no, Titus!" Words like that will make you pick up your pace. You will never guess what greeted me when I turned the corner. Two little boys standing on chairs they had pulled up to the counter and staring, with eyes the size of saucers, at a toaster engulfed in flames. "What happened?" I screamed as I ran over to them, unplugging the toaster, opening the back door, and tossing the blazing metal out in the rain. After a few minutes of calming down (me, not the boys; they clearly weren't afraid), I figured out what happened. Ethan found batteries and gave them to Titus, who thought it would be a fantastic idea to toast them like he had seen Mom make toast many times before. What they didn't expect was for the toaster to catch on fire. But thank the Lord I woke up when I did, or the story might have ended differently.

The team laughed at the story I shared and asked if they could feature it in the magazine. A little starstruck, I agreed and excitedly waited for the issue to be released. My excitement quickly faded when the issue arrived at my house, as it likened my boys to a popular, destructive, and inappropriate group of reality TV celebrities. Awesome. I told my mom to grab a copy featuring her precious grandsons. We laugh about it now, but that instance and many more made me realize I will never write a book on parenting. It's a jungle out here, and this parenting gig is not for the faint of heart. That I am confident about.

Watching the Olympics is one of our favorite things to do as a family. We might be a little obsessed, to the point of creating our own Estes Olympics. Our house gets an Olympic-themed makeover, we create events for our family to compete in, and we crown the winners with medals. It's incredible and intense, but that's how we roll in the Estes household. As we sit on the couch cheering for the athletes as they compete, we can't help but notice a common theme with their demeanor. They carry themselves with confidence. Some are a little cockier than others, but each athlete appears honored to represent their country and compete. Why are they confident? Because they have prepared for the event. It wasn't a spur-of-the-moment decision that led to anxiety over their performance abilities. No, they spent hours, months, and years training and preparing for their event. Their preparation led to their confidence.

My desire is for you to have confidence too. Unlike how I felt with my parenting, I want you to be prepared. Negative scripts may be a common practice in your mind. That's OK. But while these scripts can be scary and damaging, you can confidently change them. That's why I wrote this book. It's time for you to train and prepare, to use this guide for what to do when you feel those scripts try to creep in. You aren't unprepared and helpless. No, you are equipped and ready.

Days may come when you struggle to remember what you've learned, and that's OK. Pick up this book, and check back in with the "It's Time for Your Glow Up!" sections. It's work, it takes practice, but like Nehemiah yelled out to his enemies as they tried to distract and taunt him ("I am doing a great work and I cannot come down. Why should the work stop while I leave it and come down to you?" [Neh. 6:3 ESV]), you, bestie, are doing good work, the work that brings freedom, breaks chains, and changes lives. Don't get distracted, and don't stop. Build confidence as you continue the work.

OK, if I haven't shocked you enough in this book, try this on for size. In my senior year of high school, I decided to compete in the school's beauty pageant. The pageant was more of a glorified popularity contest, where model-worthy beautiful girls sang and pranced around for all to see. That sounded like a fun opportunity for the average girl whose singing made dogs howl. I could have a little fun and shake things up. Did I want to win the competition? Of course. But first and foremost, I desired to have fun and make new friends. They asked questions like "What is your favorite food?" Macaroni and cheese: solid answer. I sauntered across the stage in my bubblegum-pink dress adorned with thousands of crystals, with my hunky tux-wearing boyfriend by my side. Spoiler alert: that boyfriend is now my hunky husband. Well played, high school Brittany; well played.

When the time came for the talent portion, I did the only thing I knew to do: storytelling. My high school years were spent on a competitive acting team where my signature event had always been storytelling. The idea behind the event was to make a children's book come to life. I created locations and scenes, and I embodied each character to tell my story. My only prop was a single chair. Nothing brought me joy like storytelling did. So that night, I took the stage, explained to the audience the greatness they were about to behold, and put on a show. This particular book involved me on all fours mooing like a constipated cow—real glamorous pageant material right there! One of the other characters was a magical genie who piped up with his trademark line each time he granted a wish. I'd strike a pose, with a finger pointed to the sky while I channeled my best disco vibes, and yell something along the lines of, "I've got the power!" at the top of my lungs. The crowd, which was witnessing something never done on the pageant stage, roared with laughter. In the shock of a lifetime, I won the pageant that year. Shoot, I swept the entire event—I won Miss Congeniality and tied for Best Talent. Who would have ever thought? A girl who decided to play the game the only way she knew how, as fully herself, won.

Take a lesson from high school Brittany. The best person to be is yourself. Play the game the only way you know how to, the way God created you to. But even more than that, I want you to know that you have the power. You have the power to flip the script and reframe the narrative of your mind. If you need a laugh or little reminder to keep trying, just picture me singing this over you: *You've got the power!* Or you can call me and I'll do it. Your girl isn't afraid; I just believe in you that much.

I'm not exactly sure why, but this book feels harder for me to write and close. Frankly, I was a little intimidated, because I understand the weight these words hold. Over the past couple of months, I've been gifted the chance to see my previous piece of work change lives right in front of me. But with you, my new besties, it feels a little different. While there's a weight to this message, there's also a glimmer of hope. Because I know what this could mean for you, your life, and your future. I also know this truth: your generation is like none that have come before. You are something special. Jackie Hill Perry, a famous author and speaker, said this about your generation on a podcast: "When these cats believe in something, they'll fight for it." I believe this with my whole heart. You hold the key to the future, and you will become unstoppable in your pursuits of helping others flip their scripts.

As I finish, Kari Jobe's "The Blessing" is playing in the background, tears still streaming down my face as I'm still crying out to God on your behalf. I want the Lord to show you favor, to bring you freedom, and for it to trickle down from your generation and to the next generation and so on. I wanted his presence to go before you and beside you, for him to be all around you as you work to reframe the narrative in your mind and allow God's truth to saturate it completely.

This is freedom for your generation, for the ones behind you, and for those who follow. It's something we've laughed together about and cried over, and hopefully it has caused us to mark up the pages of this book. One truth remains. Through the power of Christ in you, you have the ability to flip your script. My heart beats for you to fully comprehend this freedom, but God desires it even more.

If you were to come over to my house, have a meal, and maybe some coffee, we'd inevitably get to the heart. Don't get me wrong: I'm a party girl and am always up for a good laugh, but that can only take us so far. If we're going to be friends, I want to know your heart. This book was our living room coffee chat. Maybe one day, we can do it in person for real. Can we be besties? But until then, I hope you've felt the love of a bestie walking alongside you and cheering you on like a Dallas Cowboys cheerleader. That's a lot of cheer, in case you didn't know.

If we had our heart talk in the comfort of my home, there would be a point at which you'd need to leave. You know, because of families and lives and everything in between. I'm sad about it too. We would hug, and I'd probably snap a picture to post on "the Gram" (a.k.a. Instagram). But before you headed out, your eyes would catch a glimpse of something sparkly and fantastic displayed above my front door. It's an incredible painting my sweet friend made for me and probably one of my favorite things hanging in my home. It's above my door because I want everyone leaving my home to have this blessing imparted to them. It's like sending you off with a love note from Jesus and me. And I love every bit of it.

Since our time is up, the coffee cups are dry, and you're about to leave, here's my blessing over you as you shut this book and take on this world.

> The LORD bless you and keep you;
> the LORD make his face shine on you and be gracious to you;
> the LORD turn his face toward you
> and give you peace. (Num. 6:24–26)

Glow up, girl.
Go out and flip the script.

ACKNOWLEDGMENTS

J esus, thank you for giving me the words to share. Without you I would lead such a dull and broken life. But you have shown me how to shine and give it all I've got!

Sam—How did I get so lucky? There were many days when I tried to wave my white flag and call it quits with this book because life was a lot, and quitting seemed easier. But you wouldn't let me do it. Thank you for believing in me and being my ultimate hype team—even to the point of barricading me in my room so I'd meet my deadline while feeding me H-E-B chips and queso and coffee. You know the way to my heart.

My kids (Ethan, James, Poppy, Titus, Paisley, Penelope, Pippa, Asher)—Watching you grow up is scary and yet the most fun. I know I mess things up and fail you often, but I want you to know that I couldn't love you more. I'm so proud of each of you. These words were written with you in mind. You are world changers; now go do your thing!

Ron and Tina (Mom and Dad)—Thank you for embracing my quirkiness and encouraging me to shine. When I look back on my teenage years now as an adult/parent, I'm so thankful for your influence and truth. Our house was full of fun and Jesus. You shaped me and because of that helped me see how best to encourage others. This book is birthed from the foundation you built in my life and your legacy lived out. Thank you.

Allison—What can't you do? Seriously, you are THE most talented person I know. You breathe life into everything you touch, this book included. Seriously, this cover is what dreams are made of! There was so much you did for my last book that went unseen by most, and that is where I failed you. I am FOREVER on team Allison and will champion you until I can't cheer anymore. Thank you for using your gifts in the most glorious ways. My life is better because I get to see you bring out the God-colors in this world like only you can do.

Ever—You were a WHOLE QUEEN on the cover of this book. Thank you for saying yes to being the face of this book. You, my dear, are stunning—but beyond looks, it's the joy and life that radiates from you. Never let anyone change your glow or try to dim your light. Be ALL IN for life and who God created you to be.

Heather and Mama Gerry—You prayed this book into existence. Quite literally, it would not be what it is without you in the background, praying me through it. Thank you for loving me well and speaking truth over me when I needed it most.

Jason, Duane, and the Leafwood team—You have believed in me and my words from the start. It's been an incredible journey, and I feel so blessed to have a team that listens and trusts my vision. This book is more than a bottom line to you; it's a ministry. You lead in a way that reminds me what we do is for the Kingdom and what a gift it is. Thankful for your friendship and the heart you pour into all you do.

CONNECT WITH BRITTANY

Brittany is passionate about people. She wants everyone to be a "bestie" and would love to hear from you if you want to email her at jbrittanyestes@gmail.com. You can continue the fun by following her on Instagram, TikTok, and Facebook, @jbrittanyestes.

Like she said in her book, here's her cell phone number if you want to give her a call: (601) 706-9851.

Brittany is a life coach. She specializes in helping people of all ages, including teens, find breakthrough, purpose, and direction in their lives. If you're interested in booking a session with her, you can find out more at brittanyestes.com/coaching. She is also available to inspire and engage your church, team, or audience. Brittany is a dynamic speaker who has spoken all across the country, bringing her unique perspective and exciting storytelling with her. If you're interested in having Brittany come to your next event, check out brittanyestes.com/speak.

notes